Economics for People and the Planet

T0161464

Economics for People and the Planet

Inequality in the Era of Climate Change

James K. Boyce

ANTHEM PRESS

Anthem Press
An imprint of Wimbledon Publishing Company
www.anthempress.com

This edition first published in UK and USA 2019
by ANTHEM PRESS
75–76 Blackfriars Road, London SE1 8HA, UK
or PO Box 9779, London SW19 7ZG, UK
and
244 Madison Ave #116, New York, NY 10016, USA

First published in the UK and USA by Anthem Press 2019

British Library Cataloguing-in-Publication Data
A catalogue record for this book is available from the British Library.

ISBN-13: 978-1-78527-134-2 (Pbk)
ISBN-10: 1-78527-134-2 (Pbk)

This title is also available as an e-book.

CONTENTS

ILLUSTRATIONS

Figures

Tables

ACKNOWLEDGEMENTS

I am grateful to Tej Sood and Abi Pandey at Anthem Press and to series editors Kevin Gallagher and Jayati Ghosh for encouraging me to bring these essays together in a book. Special thanks to Alejandro Reuss, Chris Sturr and Tim Wise, who published a number of these pieces at *TripleCrisis*, and to Chris Cox, my excellent editor at *Harper's* magazine. I thank Arpita Biswas for her valuable assistance in preparation of the manuscript. It is also a pleasure to thank the colleagues with whom several of the essays were co-authored: Peter Barnes (chapter 5), Klara Zwickl and Michael Ash (chapter 14), Manuel Pastor (chapter 16) and Matthew Riddle (chapter 25).

Part I
RETHINKING ECONOMICS AND THE ENVIRONMENT

Chapter 1

LIMITS TO GROWTH – OF WHAT?

Environmentalism needs a new banner: Grow the good and shrink the bad.

Average national income is a notoriously imperfect measure of the average person's well-being. The 2010 BP oil spill in the Gulf of Mexico – with clean-up and damage costs of $90 billion – added about $300 to the average American's 'income'. But it added nothing to the nation's well-being. The world's most expensive prison system, costing almost $40 billion per year, adds another $125 per person. This doesn't make the country's residents better off than people living in countries that don't incarcerate one in every 100 adults.[1]

Of course, national income includes many good things, too. Growing food and building homes add to national income. So does public spending on education and healthcare. Unlike oil spills and jails, these really do add to human well-being.

Along with good stuff and bad stuff, national income includes a third category of stuff that is just useless – goods and services that neither add to our well-being nor subtract from it but still get counted in the income pie. A prime example is what the economist Thorstein Veblen called 'conspicuous consumption' – items consumed not for their intrinsic worth but simply to impress other people and jockey for a higher rung on society's pecking order. These goods and services have zero net effect on national well-being, since for every person who climbs a rung, someone else slips one.

Of course, not all bad or useless things are counted as national income. But neither are all good things. Unpaid work caring for children, the elderly and the disabled doesn't count. Clean air, clean water and climate stability don't count. Free, open-source information and culture don't count.

The national income pie is an odd subset of the good, the bad and the useless. All three slices get lumped together when economists tell us that average income in the United States is roughly $56,000 per person.

Researchers in the emerging field called 'happiness studies' have devised other ways to measure well-being. They find that beyond the level of income that is needed to satisfy basic wants, such as food and shelter, there is little or

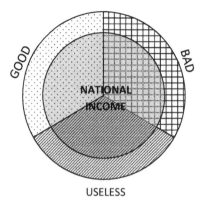

USELESS

Figure 1.1 National income: The good, the bad and the useless

National income (or GDP), denoted by the dark inner circle, counts everything with a price tag no matter whether it's good, bad or useless. At the same time, it omits some good things that enhance our well-being as well as some bad things that diminish it. So growth of national income is not a reliable measure of economic progress. Our goal instead should be to grow the good and shrink the bad.

no correlation between a country's average income and the happiness of the average person. Past some threshold, increases in the good and bad appear to cancel each other out, and the useless slice of the income pie can get pretty fat.

Since national income isn't the same as well-being, growth in national income isn't the same as improvement in well-being. All too often, this crucial distinction gets lost in acrimonious debates about the relationship between the economy and the environment (see Figure 1.1).

Forty years ago, a report called *The Limits to Growth* drew attention to the indisputable fact that our planet does not have an infinite capacity to serve as a source for raw materials and a sink for waste disposal.[2] In choosing to call this idea the 'limits to growth', however, the authors fell into a rhetorical trap that has haunted environmentalism ever since.

The problem is that most people believe that growth is good. When they think about the national income pie, they think about the good slice, unlike environmentalists who think about the bad slice.

Because they're really talking about different things, proponents and opponents of growth often talk right past each other. And when they assume that the good and bad are inseparable, both sides buy into the myth that there is an inexorable tradeoff between economic well-being and environmental quality. If the good and the bad must go together, they must grow together.

The result: growth wins, and environmentalists play damage control.

To find a way out of this impasse, we need better measures of economic well-being, better public policies and better language.

A growing number of economists recognize the need to develop new measures of well-being that count the good as positive, subtract the bad as negative, and ignore the useless. In 2009, the Commission on the Measurement of Economic Performance and Social Progress, chaired by Joseph Stiglitz, Amartya Sen and Jean-Paul Fitoussi, produced a powerful and wide-ranging critique of the conventional measure of national income.[3] In the United States, dozens of state-level initiatives are now experimenting with different ways to measure well-being.

In the policy arena, we need to both advance human well-being and protect the environment on which it ultimately rests. This requires not only sound regulations but also true-cost prices to orient investment and consumption decisions to the full range of costs and benefits. In climate policy, for example, although regulations such as fuel economy standards for automobiles can help to promote the clean energy transition, in the absence of a price on carbon emissions there will always be strong incentives to burn cheap fossil fuels.

Last but not least, we need better language. We need to move beyond the stale 'pro-growth' versus 'anti-growth' rhetoric of the past. It's time to raise a new banner: *Grow the good and shrink the bad.*

Chapter 2

THE TWIN TRAGEDIES OF OPEN ACCESS

Open access – in the sense of a complete absence of property rights and regulations – leads not only to the abuse of natural resources but also to the abuse of the poor by the rich. Climate change is a case in point.

To combat global warming, we must confront two tragedies of open access. The first is sometimes called the 'tragedy of the commons', a misnomer since societies often devise rules to manage common property sustainably. This tragedy is that when there is open access to a scarce resource, individuals have no incentive to conserve it and instead will overexploit it even to the point of collapse. In the case of climate change, the scarce resource is the limited capacity of the biosphere to absorb and recycle our emissions of carbon dioxide and other greenhouse gases.

The second tragedy of open access is less widely recognized but no less real. Although in theory open-access resources are equally available to all, in practice some people are, in George Orwell's haunting phrase, 'more equal than others'. Open access often generates short-run benefits for those who least need them and long-run costs for those who can least afford them. Global warming is a good example. Rich countries burn more fossil fuels than do poor countries, generating more carbon dioxide emissions. And within any given country, richer people benefit most from the fossil-fuelled economy by virtue of the fact that they consume more goods and services.

Meanwhile, it is poor countries and poor people who stand to bear the greatest costs of global warming. They are less able to invest in air conditioners, sea walls and other adaptations. They live closer to the edge: while the rich can weather a 20 per cent decline in their real incomes with relative ease, for the poor the same decline may push them over the margin between life and death. And the places that climate models show will be hit hardest by global warming – including drought-prone regions of sub-Saharan Africa and typhoon-vulnerable South and South East Asia – are home to some of the world's poorest people.

Effective climate solutions will demand that we address both tragedies. At the international level, the key to a comprehensive agreement to reduce emissions is the principle that every person in the world has an equal right to the planet's limited carbon-storage capacity. In exempting developing countries from emission targets, the Kyoto Protocol implicitly embraced this principle. But by basing its targets for industrialized countries on past emissions, the agreement instead rewarded countries for their past pollution. To craft an accord that is acceptable to all nations, it will be necessary to build it around the principle of equal carbon entitlements.

Does this mean that the majority of people in the industrialized countries must endure a cut in their standards of living to safeguard the global environment? Not if the same egalitarian principle is applied *within* countries, too. The creation of national 'sky trusts' that receive revenue from carbon taxes or the sale of carbon permits to firms that bring fossil fuels into the economy, and then recycle the money equally to every woman, man and child, would protect the real incomes of lower-income and middle-income households. The cost of carbon taxes or permits ultimately are passed to consumers: households pay the price, with the amount per household depending on its carbon footprint. Upper-income households, who generally consume the most, will pay the most; low-income households generally will pay the least. Since everyone receives the same carbon dividend, households that consume less than the average come out ahead financially. Because in every country income and consumption are skewed towards the rich, carbon-revenue recycling protects the purchasing power of the middle class and raises the real incomes of the poor.

Policies that combine environmental protection with income protection for the majority of the world's people are not only ethically desirable but also politically necessary to ensure broad and durable public support for the fight against global climate change.

Chapter 3

PURSUING PROFITS – OR POWER?

In corporations, the pursuit of power often trumps the pursuit of profits.

Do corporations seek to maximize profits? Or do they seek to maximize power? The two may be complementary – wealth begets power, power begets wealth – but they're not the same. One important difference is that profits can come from an expanding economic 'pie', whereas the power often is a zero-sum game: more for me means less for you. And for corporations, the pursuit of power sometimes trumps the pursuit of profits.

Power versus Profits

Take public education, for example. Greater investment in education from pre-school through college could increase the overall pie of economic well-being. But it also would narrow the educational advantage of corporate oligarchs and their privately schooled children – and diminish the power that comes with it. Although corporations could benefit from the bigger pie produced by a better-educated labor force, there's a tension between what's good for business and what's good for the business elite.

Similarly, the business elite often supports economic austerity instead of full-employment policies that would increase growth and profits. This may have something to do with the fact that austerity widens inequality, while full employment narrows it by empowering workers. If we peel away the layers of the onion, at the core again we find that those at the top of the corporate pyramid put power before profits.

As one more example, consider the politics of government regulation. Corporations routinely pass along to consumers whatever costs they incur as a result of regulation. In the automobile industry, for instance, the regulations that mandated seat belts, catalytic converters and better fuel efficiency added a few hundred dollars to the price of a vehicle. They didn't cut automaker profit margins. If the costs are ultimately borne by consumers, why do regulations face such stiff resistance from the corporations? The answer may have less to do with profits than with power. Corporate chieftains are touchy about their 'management prerogatives'. They simply don't like other folks telling them what to do.

Corporate Power versus Government Power

In a famous 1971 memorandum to the US Chamber of Commerce, future Supreme Court Justice Lewis Powell wrote, 'The day is long past when the chief executive office of a major corporation discharges his responsibility by maintaining a satisfactory growth of profits.' To counter what he described as an attack on the American free-enterprise system by labour unions, students and consumer advocates, Powell urged CEOs to act on 'the lesson that political power is necessary; that power must be assiduously cultivated; and that when necessary, it must be used aggressively and with determination'.[1] He was preaching to a receptive choir.

The idea that firms single-mindedly maximize profits is an axiom of faith in today's orthodox Econ 101, but alternative theories have a long history in the broader economics profession. Thorstein Veblen, John Maynard Keynes and Fred Hirsch all saw an individual's position *relative* to others as a key motivation in economic behavior. A sound-bite version of this idea is encountered on bumper stickers: 'He Who Dies with the Most Toys Wins'.

In his 1972 presidential address to the American Economics Association, titled 'Power and the Useful Economist', John Kenneth Galbraith juxtaposed the crucial role of power in the real-world economy to its neglect in orthodox economics: 'In eliding power – in making economics a nonpolitical subject – neoclassical theory [...] destroys its relation with the real world.'[2]

On the free-marketeer end of the ideological spectrum, the pursuit of power reappears but is depicted as a pathology entirely distinctive to the State. Chicago school economist William Niskanen theorized that public-sector bureaucrats seek to maximize the size of their budgets, taking this as a proxy for 'salary, perquisites of the office, public reputation, power, patronage, ease of managing the bureau, and ease of making changes'. He called this 'the peculiar economics of bureaucracy'.[3]

The pursuit of power is not unique to government bureaucracies, however. It is commonplace in corporate bureaucracies, too. In his presidential address, Galbraith made the connection: 'Between public and private bureaucracies – between GM and the Department of Transportation, between General Dynamics and the Pentagon – there is a deeply symbiotic relationship.'

Democracy versus Oligarchy

Recognizing the real-world pursuit of power not only helps us understand behaviour that otherwise may seem peculiar but also redirects our attention

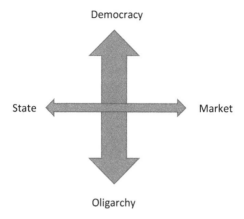

Democracy

State ← → Market

Oligarchy

Figure 3.1 The democracy-oligarchy and market-state continuums
The difference between democracy and oligarchy is not the same as the difference between the market and the state. In the absence of a democratic distribution of power, neither the market nor the state can ensure outcomes beneficial to the majority of people.

from the dichotomy between the market and the state toward the more fundamental divide between oligarchy and democracy.

Real-world societies lie somewhere on a continuum between the hypothetical extremes of absolute democracy (here taken to mean a perfectly equal distribution of power) and absolute oligarchy (a one-person dictatorship), as well as on a continuum between the polar extremes of an economy ruled only by the market or only by the state (see Figure 3.1).

In the nineteenth and twentieth centuries, contending ideologies on the 'right' and 'left' often sought to conflate these two continuums into a single axis, the right identifying the market with democracy and the state with oligarchy, the left making the opposite equation. In reality, the two axes are different.

Much ink, and even blood, has been spilled in disputes over the proper balance between the market and the state as ways to run the economy. But where a society is situated on the democracy-oligarchy axis arguably is more important for the welfare of its people. History has demonstrated that when power and wealth are concentrated in few hands, neither markets nor states can be relied upon to generate good outcomes for everyone else.

If it is natural that corporations pursue power, then it is equally natural that sustaining a democratic society requires public vigilance and action to hold their power in check.

Chapter 4

RENT IN A WARMING WORLD

To combat climate change, we need to shift from extractive rent to protective rent.

What's rent got to do with climate change? More than you might think.

Rent isn't just the monthly check that a tenant writes to her landlord. Economists use the term 'rent seeking' to mean using political and economic power to get a larger share of the national pie, rather than to grow the pie. In the United States, Nobel laureate Joseph Stiglitz observes, such dysfunctional activity has metastasized alongside deepening inequality.[1]

When rent inspires investment in useful things like housing, it's *productive*. The economic pie grows, and the society gets something in return. When rent leads to investment in unproductive activities, like lobbying to capture wealth without creating it, it's *parasitic*. The society gets nothing in return.

Two other types of rent originate in nature rather than investment. *Extractive* rent comes from nature as a source of raw materials. The difference between the selling price of crude oil and the cost of pumping it from the ground is an example.

Protective rent comes from charging for the use of nature as a sink for our wastes. In the northeastern states of the United States, for example, the Regional Greenhouse Gas Initiative requires power plants to buy carbon permits at quarterly auctions. In this way, power companies pay rent to park carbon dioxide emissions in the atmosphere. Similarly, pollution taxes now account for more than 5 per cent of government revenue in some European countries. When polluters pay to use nature's sinks, they use them less than when they're free, helping to prevent their overuse and abuse.

Extractive and protective rents both originate in nature, but they differ sharply in that one promotes resource depletion, the other conservation. The tension between these two types of rent from nature is increasingly evident in our warming world.

A daunting obstacle to climate policy arises from the vested interests of fossil fuel corporations in continuing to reap extractive rent. The value of the world's oil, coal and natural gas reserves has been estimated at $27 trillion.

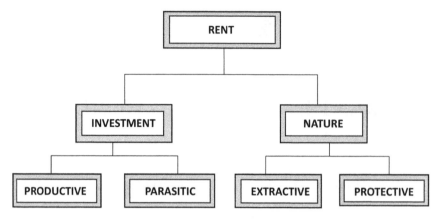

Figure 4.1 Types of rent
Rent is a payment received by owners of an asset for its use. Assets can originate in investment or in nature. Rent can be further subdivided into four types. Productive rent inspires investment in useful things. Parasitic rent inspires investment in unproductive activities. Extractive rent comes from the depletion of natural assets. Protective rent comes from the conservation of natural assets.

Much of this will have to be written off if we phase out fossil fuels. 'You can have a healthy fossil-fuel balance sheet, or a relatively healthy planet,' Bill McKibben observes. 'You can't have both.'[2]

Creating protective rent by capping or taxing carbon emissions will shrink extractive rent. The fossil fuel corporations that capture extractive rent have shown themselves willing to fight hard to defend it. But the question of who will receive climate-protective rent – and who will fight for it – remains up in the air.

One possibility is to return the protective rent to the people via equal per capita dividends – a policy known as 'cap and dividend' in the case of permits or 'fee and dividend' in the case of taxes.[3] Another possibility is to give free permits to polluters and let them pocket the rent as windfall profits – a policy known as 'cap and trade' but more accurately termed 'cap and giveaway'. A third option is to let the government keep the money, as in the case of Europe's green taxes (see Figure 4.1).

Dividend proponents argue that recycling rent to the people is necessary to secure durable public support for climate policy as fossil fuel prices rise during the decades-long clean energy transition. Cap-and-giveaway proponents argue that surrendering the rent to fossil fuel corporations is necessary to neutralize their opposition to climate policy.

Underlying these strategies are fundamentally different beliefs about who owns nature's sinks, as well as about politics. Dividends are based on the principle that the gifts of nature belong to everyone equally. Cap and giveaway is based on the premise that the same corporations that today profit from extracting nature's wealth ought to be paid in the future – or must be bribed – to leave it in the ground.

Dividends make sense if we believe that it's possible to enact a policy that benefits the majority of people financially as well as environmentally. Cap and giveaway makes sense if we believe that might makes right, and that the power of the people can never match the power of the corporations. But the serial defeats suffered by cap-and-trade bills in Washington in the first decade of this century cast doubt on the political realism of this 'realpolitik' environmentalism.[4] When the chips were down, the fossil fuel industry proved unwilling to buy into the new-rent-for-old deal.

The only way we will see a switch from extractive rents for corporations to protective rents for the public will be if ordinary people join together to make it happen. The democratic politics that this would demand may seem like a quaint idea in the political climate of the early twenty-first century. But nothing less is required. To change the nature of the rent we get from nature, we must change who gets it.

Chapter 5

UNIVERSAL ASSETS FOR UNIVERSAL INCOME

Universal basic income can come from universal basic assets – our common wealth.

Lately there has been renewed discussion of universal income: regular cash payments to everyone regardless of race, gender or need. In the United States, variants on this idea were earlier proposed by people as ideologically diverse as the revolutionary Tom Paine, civil rights leader Martin Luther King Jr., free-market economist Milton Friedman and President Richard Nixon. Renewed interest has been sparked today by the income stagnation experienced by America's middle class and working poor, and by the persistent slow growth experienced by the economy.

The idea finds support across America's ideological spectrum, in an era when hardly anything else does. Liberals, or at least some of them, like it as a way to preserve the middle class when jobs no longer pay enough. Conservatives, or at least some of them, like it as a way to reduce dependence on our byzantine maze of welfare programmes.[1]

But universal income would be expensive, and it quickly runs into the stumbling block of how to pay for it. Its widespread appeal is held in check by equally widespread aversion to taxes, especially taxation for the purpose of redistributing income. Fortunately, there's another way to pay for it: universal *income* can come from universal *assets*, a.k.a. our common wealth.

The common wealth that we inherit together and create together is worth trillions of dollars, yet at present we derive little, if any, income from it. Our joint inheritance includes gifts of nature such as the atmosphere, underground minerals and fresh water, as well as socially created assets like our legal and financial infrastructure, without which private corporations couldn't exist much less thrive. If these were better managed, our common assets could pay a universal monthly dividend to every American, children included.

Consider, for example, the limited capacity of the Earth's atmosphere to absorb safely the pollutants that cause climate change. By charging polluters for use of this scarce asset, we can both protect our climate and generate dividends for all. Other forms of pollution can and should be priced, too. And we could charge market prices for extracting minerals and timber from public lands, resources now leased to private firms cheaply in sweetheart deals.[2] Making polluters and extractors pay for their use of natural assets, without abandoning smart regulations, would provide market-based incentives for their wise use.

Universal assets include gifts of society as well as gifts of nature. An example is the legal and financial infrastructure that underpins the economy, without which the private fortunes of billionaires would be impossible.

Here's how investor Warren Buffett once made this point to Barack Obama: 'I was lucky enough to be born in a time and place where society values my talent, and gave me a good education to develop that talent, and set up the laws and the financial system to let me do what I love doing – and make a lot of money doing it.'[3] Buffett acknowledges that society is responsible for 'a very significant percentage' of his wealth.[4] Nobel economist Herbert Simon was more precise:

If we're very generous with ourselves, I suppose we might claim we 'earned' as much as one-fifth of our income. The rest is patrimony associated with being a member of an enormously productive social system.[5]

Currently, those who benefit the most from socially built assets pay little or nothing to use them. But that needn't be the case. We could charge for using key components of our legal and financial infrastructure. Modest transaction fees on trades of stocks, bonds and derivatives, for example, could generate more than $300 billion per year.[6] Such fees would not only generate income for everyone; they would also discourage speculation, helping to stabilize the financial system. Similar fees could be applied to patent and royalty earnings, which are returns not only to individual innovation but also to the monopoly rights to innovations that society provides.

Here's the bottom line. It would not be difficult to create a portfolio of universal assets that could pay, say, $200 a month to every US resident. The money could be wired automatically to everyone's bank accounts or debit cards with minimal administrative bureaucracy. It would be received by everyone as joint owners of our universal assets; it would be paid by users of these assets in proportion to their use. The payments would not be taxes collected by the government but rather payments to owners – all of us – for the value generated by *our* assets.

If everyone receives regular income from common assets, will anyone have an incentive to work? Certainly, $200 a month wouldn't be enough to live on in the United States. And unless the universal asset-based income was improbably high, most people would still want to work to earn better livelihoods. If the universal income was high enough, some people might be freed from the need to do work they really hate, but that's a good thing. Others might be freed to do work they really love, even if it doesn't pay all that much.[7] That's a good thing, too.

In the game *Monopoly*, $200 is the amount every player gets for passing 'Go'. Such cash infusions aren't bad for the game: they help all players to compete. The same will happen in the economy if everyone gets infusions of $200 a month. The extra money would relieve some burdens of working families, heighten life chances for success and satisfaction, and stimulate the economy.

But the gifts of nature and society will not come to us as gifts from our political leaders. We will win rights to universal basic assets only if we join together to claim them. Fittingly, we will have to earn them by using another asset that Americans won the same way: democracy.

Chapter 6

UNIVERSAL BASIC INCOME: SIX QUESTIONS

Basic questions on universal basic income: an interview with Vita International.

A basic income would not be cheap – depending on how the programme was structured. But how feasible is universal basic income (UBI) to implement in reality?

Funding for UBI is the main obstacle to implementing it. One way to do so would be to charge for use of common wealth (such as the limited ability of the environment to safely absorb pollution) and to return the revenue to the people. In this case, UBI would come from assets whose ownership is universal, too.

But what about the worry that a universal basic income would stop people from working? How would UBI affect labour supply?

It is unlikely that UBI would be large enough to deter people from working. It would, however, give them greater freedom to choose work they want to do, including work that doesn't pay as much but has richer non-monetary rewards.

Another major question is whether UBI is designed to supplement or substitute for currently existing welfare programmes. What do you believe?

UBI could either supplement or substitute for current welfare programmes. Most likely it would do some of both.

A recent study estimates that 47 per cent of US jobs potentially will be replaced by robots and automated technology in the next 10 to 20 years.[1] Is universal basic income an answer to automation?

Automation is one of many factors that contribute to unemployment and underemployment. By providing an additional source of income, UBI would help to provide a cushion against the various factors that erode income from labour.

Low-paid, part-time, temporary and seasonal workers would get a big boost to their incomes. Many people might use the payment to invest time and money in education or training. Many experts argue that universal basic income would help to fight poverty and inequalities.

There is no panacea to the problems of poverty and inequality, but UBI would be a step in the right direction.

Some say entrepreneurship would become less risky. How?

Much as UBI would provide a cushion against unemployment and under-employment, it would cushion would-be entrepreneurs against risk of low incomes. This might make it easier to start small businesses.

Chapter 7

ENVIRONMENTALISM'S ORIGINAL SIN

Humans-versus-nature is a dead end.

In 2007 the National Audubon Society, one of the leading environmental organizations in the United States, issued a report headlined 'Common Birds in Decline'. Based on statistical analysis of 40 years of bird population data, it announced the alarming decline of many of our most common and beloved birds.[1]

The story attracted wide press coverage. 'Spreading suburbs and large-scale farming are contributing to a precipitous decline in once common meadow birds,' began a story in the *New York Times*.[2] An accompanying editorial lamented, 'We somehow trusted that all the innocent little birds were here to stay. What they actually need to survive, it turns out, is a landscape that is less intensely human.'[3] A letter to the editor predicted that the deadly pattern will continue 'as long as we ask the earth to support too many people'.[4]

Few commentators bothered to study the study itself.[5] Had they done so, they would have found some more upbeat news, as well. They might have noted, for example, that among 309 bird species for which statistically meaningful trends could be established from the data in two population surveys, birds showing a 'large increase' in numbers exceeded those showing a 'large decrease'. Forty-one species recorded a large increase in both of the surveys; only twelve saw a large decrease.

Looking at the data on individual species, reported in an appendix to the study, readers would have found that one species registering a large increase was the bald eagle, until recently classified as endangered in the lower 48 states. The eagle's numbers rebounded after the 1972 ban on use of the pesticide DDT. Another rapidly increasing species is the wild turkey, extirpated in many north-eastern states more than a century ago by forest clearing for agriculture. It has returned as abandonment of farms led to forest regrowth. In both cases, the comebacks were actively abetted by private and governmental restoration initiatives.

Of the species that registered significant declines, many are birds of open habitats – meadows, pastures and early successional forests – habitats that were created and sustained by farmers in the eighteenth and nineteenth centuries on lands that have now reverted to forest.

So the take-home messages from the Audubon study could have been the following:

- More bird species in the United States are increasing in population than decreasing.
- Efforts to protect and restore threatened species have scored some major successes.
- Many of the species whose numbers are declining depend on types of human-created habitats that are disappearing.

The relationship between non-industrial agriculture and biodiversity is not unique to birds in the north-eastern United States. For example, in a study in the northern highlands of Oaxaca, Mexico, researchers have found that widespread abandonment of traditional *milpa* agriculture is leading to 'localised declines in biodiversity, despite (or because of) extensive forest resurgence'.[6]

The American writer Wallace Stegner once observed that when facts enter 'the maw of that great machine that at once creates and obeys public opinion', they often come out as something else. 'Ideas,' he wrote, 'are like dye thrown into moving water.'[7]

A powerful current in American environmentalism maintains that humans are bad for nature. It is a belief that took hold with the closing of the frontier in the late nineteenth century, but its roots can be traced to early European settlers' misperception of North America as a pristine wilderness, and perhaps even further back to the Christian doctrine of 'original sin'.[8]

The mission of environmentalists in this story is to preach self-restraint in a valiant effort to curb our ecological footprint and limit our misdeeds so as to remain within Nature's capacity for forgiveness.

Absent from this narrative are the ways that humans can and do have positive impacts on the environment. Call it our ecological handprint. It can be seen in the diverse habitats created and sustained by non-industrial agriculture. It can be seen in the co-evolutionary processes by which humans domesticated plants and animals, originating the species on which we depend today for most of our food. It can be seen in the ecological restoration that brought the return of the wild turkey and bald eagle.

Hellfire and brimstone may be effective for garnering media attention and procuring donations from the faithful and fearful. But original-sin environmentalism not only rests on a selective reading of our past; it also has led to a political dead end. When the choice is framed as Humans versus Nature, it turns out that most people will choose Humans. If environmentalism is to win the future, we must move beyond this false dichotomy.

Chapter 8

RETHINKING EXTINCTION

In the space of a single century, the passenger pigeon went from being the world's most abundant bird to complete extinction. What happened to it – and to us?

A little more than a hundred years ago, a bird named Martha, the last surviving passenger pigeon, died in the Cincinnati Zoo. Her death was remarkable in the annals of extinction not only because we know its precise date – 1 September 1914 – but also because only decades earlier the passenger pigeon had been the most abundant bird on Earth. Martha's demise helped to transform American beliefs about our relationship with nature, and the bird became an icon in the environmental movement, which was emerging just as she died.

Among the many billions of passenger pigeons who predeceased Martha was her cage mate, George, who died in 1910. The pair were named after Martha and George Washington. In the century that separated the first First Lady from the last passenger pigeon, America's economy went through a profound transformation. The country's population increased more than tenfold, and average income more than quadrupled. Only 6 per cent of Americans lived in cities when Martha Washington died, in 1802. In 1914, the number was closer to 50 per cent. The passenger pigeon's extinction was bound up with these changes, and what happened to the bird tells us much about what happened – and is still happening – to us.

Tourists came from near and far to see Martha after George's death. The aerial displays of passenger pigeons had astonished their parents and grandparents, but at the zoo they found a pathetic creature with 'drooping wings, atremble with the palsy of extreme old age', in the words of a reporter.[1] To dissuade the public from flinging sand at her to make her move, the zookeepers roped off her cage.

After her death, Martha was frozen in a 300-pound block of ice and shipped to the Smithsonian Institution, in Washington. Her internal organs were removed and preserved in the museum's 'wet collections', and her skin was stuffed and mounted for display. In 1977, when the Cincinnati Zoo opened a passenger-pigeon memorial, Martha was flown in for the dedication cere-mony. She travelled first class.

The species at greatest risk for extinction tend to be small, geographically isolated populations: of the 140 documented bird extinctions since the six-teenth century, 133 were species found only on islands. The passenger pigeon was different. Unlike, say, the black mamo, which was endemic to the island of Molokai in the Hawaiian archipelago and went extinct around the same time, the pigeon had a range that covered most of the United States and Canada east of the Rockies, north of the Gulf of Mexico and south of Hudson Bay. And its sheer numbers were almost beyond belief.

The ornithologist Alexander Wilson, writing at the dawn of the nineteenth century, described a flock crossing the Ohio River:

A column, eight or ten miles in length, would appear from Kentucky [...] steering across to Indiana. The leaders of this great body would sometimes gradually vary their course, until it formed a large bend, of more than a mile in diameter, those behind tracing the exact route of their predecessors. This would continue sometimes long after both extremities were beyond the reach of sight, so that the whole, with its glittery undulations, marked a space on the face of the heavens resembling the windings of a vast and majestic river.[2]

Wilson estimated the number of pigeons in the flock using its density, breadth, speed and the time it took to pass overhead, and came up with a count of 2,230,272,000. In *Birds and People* (2013), Mark Cocker, a British naturalist, concludes that while this was probably an overestimate, Wilson had undoubt-edly seen 'well over a billion birds'.[3] And that was just one flock; at any given time several were likely to have existed on the continent, plus a scattering of smaller groups and individuals.

A. W. Schorger, whose 1955 monograph on the passenger pigeon is the most exhaustive – some might say obsessive – assemblage of information about the species, reckoned that its total population when Europeans first reached America was three to five billion. To put this number in perspective, the current worldwide population of rock doves – what most people recognize as pigeons – is around 260 million.

The passenger pigeon is held in tender regard by environmentalists today, but it is worth pausing to imagine the birds in their heyday. The majestic rivers in the sky could inspire not only awe but also dread. When a flock appeared in Columbus, Ohio, in the spring of 1855 and blotted out the sun, 'children screamed and ran for home', according to an account published years later in the *Columbus Dispatch*. 'Women gathered their long skirts and hurried for the shelter of stores. Horses bolted. A few people mumbled frightened words about the approach of the millennium, and several dropped on their knees and prayed.'[4]

The birds roosted and nested in enormous colonies. The largest on record, found in central Wisconsin in 1871, extended for 850 square miles. As many as 300 birds would alight in a single tree, shattering trunks and branches with an effect that was likened to that of a tornado or hurricane. The clearings the pigeons created were soon populated by species that did not thrive in dense forest. The fuel buildup from broken limbs increased the intensity of fires. Pigeon excrement altered the nutrient balance of the soil. The birds' heavy consumption of red-oak acorns is believed to have tilted the composition of eastern forests in favour of white oaks. In these respects, the passenger pigeon was a keystone species, which helped shape the ecosystems of eastern North America.

We now know that 99.9 per cent of all species that ever existed are extinct. But until the end of the eighteenth century, the idea that *any* species had gone extinct was almost unknown. Nature was seen as a steady state, an unchanging tableau, not a process. Thomas Jefferson, whose passions included natural history, put it this way:

Such is the economy of nature that no instance can be produced of her having permitted any one race of her animals to become extinct; of her having formed any link in her great work so weak as to be broken.[5]

The discovery of extinction is generally credited to Georges Cuvier, who taught at the Museum of Natural History in Paris and, in his spare time, studied the ancient bones in its collection. In 1796, Cuvier delivered a public lecture in which he announced that he had identified two lost species: the mastodon and the mammoth. By 1812, when he published a landmark four-volume treatise on fossil animals, he and others had identified 49 vanished species, including a cave bear, a pygmy hippopotamus and a pterodactyl.

Cuvier's discovery touched off a revolution in our understanding of nature that is still, in some ways, incomplete. In the years that followed his treatise, debate raged over the causes of extinction. Cuvier believed that extinctions were the result of planetary catastrophes, a view compatible with the Bible's great deluge. Within a few decades, however, an alternative view propounded by the Scottish geologist Charles Lyell had won the day. Lyell argued that extinction happened gradually, over millennia, not in cataclysmic spasms. It would not be until 1980, when a study connected the extinction of the dinosaurs to the impact of an asteroid, that the possibility of abrupt mass extinction was again taken seriously.

Scientists now recognize that both mass and gradual extinctions have occurred. Mass extinctions get more press: five of them are known to have happened so far, and some say we are now embarking on a sixth, with humans playing the part of the asteroid. Yet scientists have calculated that the Big Five together account for only 4 per cent of the extinctions that have taken place over the past 600 million years. The rest occurred in the absence of a global cataclysm.

As Elizabeth Kolbert recounts in her book, *The Sixth Extinction*, Cuvier's discovery of extinction opened the door to Darwin's discovery of evolution. If old species could disappear, maybe new species could emerge. Darwin's theory of natural selection put the two processes together. In Kolbert's words, 'Extinction and evolution were to each other the warp and weft of life's fabric.'[6] But Darwin, like Lyell, believed that the process of extinction was so gradual as to be practically imperceptible. The idea that a mass extinction could happen in our own time, and that we could cause it, required a mental leap that even Darwin wouldn't take.

The birds that most of us eat today are chickens – lots of them – and turkeys, with the occasional duck, quail or pheasant thrown in. So it is something of a shock to remember that, not so long ago, Americans were happy to eat just about anything with wings. An 1867 inventory of fowl available in the game markets of New York City and Boston featured not only wild turkeys, partridges and grouse but also robins, great blue herons, sandpipers, meadowlarks, blue jays and snow buntings.[7]

In season, passenger pigeons were especially plentiful. Alexander Wilson reported they were sometimes eaten for breakfast, lunch and dinner. The pigeon potpie – sometimes garnished with pigeon feet stuck in the middle – was common fare in colonial America. Passenger pigeons were preserved for out-of-season consumption by being salted, pickled in apple cider, smoked to make jerky, or sealed in casks with molten fat.

According to Schorger, the birds were 'a boon to the poor': in 1754, a half dozen sold in New York for a penny, a sum equivalent to 30 cents today.[8] In times of surplus, they were fed to hogs.

By the middle of the nineteenth century, railroads had connected the cities of the eastern seaboard to the great nesting colonies of the Midwest. Word of the flocks' locations spread rapidly thanks to another new technology, the telegraph, which allowed professional market hunters, as well as local amateurs, to converge on a site.

The most common way to kill passenger pigeons was to shoot them. Because the birds clustered so densely, no great skill was required to blast them from trees or out of the sky with a shotgun. Nets were widely used as well. Trappers broadcast grain and deployed captive 'stool pigeons' to attract the birds, enabling them to snare hundreds at once. Captured pigeons could be killed by crushing their skulls between the thumb and forefinger, though, as Schorger notes, 'It was difficult to continue this method without fatigue when many birds were handled.'[9] Some hunters used specially designed pliers to break the birds' necks. Others used their teeth, as Joel Greenberg recounts in

A Feathered River Across the Sky. Here's how he describes Old Joe, a one-armed Civil War veteran who netted pigeons near Petoskey, Michigan, in 1878:

> *With one motion, he would grab a pigeon by the leg and toss it into his mouth head first, then chomp down on the skull: 'What a sight! His face was smeared with blood from ear to ear; his beard dripped gore; and his clothes were covered with it.'*[10]

Dead pigeons were packed in ice, about 400 to a barrel, for shipment by rail to urban markets. A million and a half were sent south and east from the Petoskey nesting, which caused the price per barrel to fall below the cost of shipping them. For every bird that made it to the dinner table, many more were wasted. Vast numbers were left where they fell for the hogs to clean up; others spoiled in transit. As many as 10 million pigeons may have died at the Petoskey nesting altogether.

Scientists now recognize that, in addition to island species, another type of animal is especially vulnerable to extinction: those with dense colonies that attract intensive human exploitation for the market.

Not everyone was oblivious to the risk of the passenger pigeon's extinction. After witnessing the slaughter at a Kentucky roost in 1847, the French traveller Bénédict-Henry Révoil predicted that the passenger pigeon would 'simply end by disappearing from this continent' within a century. As Greenberg remarks, Révoil turned out to be 'overly optimistic by about fifty years'.[11]

To most Americans, however, the passenger pigeon seemed ridiculously abundant, and the suggestion that it could disappear was preposterous. An 1857 Ohio State Senate committee report summed up the prevailing sentiment:

> *The passenger pigeon needs no protection. Wonderfully prolific, having the vast forests of the North as its breeding grounds, traveling hundreds of miles in search of food, it is here today, and elsewhere tomorrow, and no ordinary destruction can lessen them or be missed from the myriads that are yearly produced.*[12]

The Ohio Historical Society ranked this as the fifth-most embarrassing moment in the state's history; the top spot went to the Cuyahoga River, in Cleveland, bursting into flames in 1969.

When the passenger pigeon disappeared from North America's skies, many could not believe it was really extinct and claimed that the birds had migrated to South America or Australia. Others accepted that the birds were gone but suggested that they had succumbed to some mysterious disease. Henry Ford thought they had drowned in the Pacific while attempting to fly to Asia.

In the end, it was the passenger pigeon's very abundance that probably sealed its fate. Roosting and nesting in close proximity and in vast colonies, the species exhibited the ecological survival strategy known as 'predator satiation': their numbers were sufficient to weather any losses to weasels, raccoons, hawks and other predators. Since the pigeons moved frequently, predator populations in any one place could never grow to the point that they posed an existential threat.

But in the hunters of the nineteenth century, the passenger pigeon encountered a predator that could not be satiated. The last passenger pigeon killed in the wild is generally believed to have been shot by a boy in Pike County, Ohio, on 24 March 1900. The bird was stuffed by the wife of a retired sheriff (some say the sheriff shot it himself and invented the boy as a cover story) and was named Buttons for the black shoe buttons she used to cover the holes where the eyes had been. Today Buttons is displayed at the Ohio History Center, in Columbus. Greenberg uncovered evidence of a later specimen shot in Indiana in 1902 that was destroyed when rain breached the roof of the woodshed attic where it was stored.

The extinction sparked a range of emotions. Rewards were offered for the discovery of survivors. 'No better example of eternal hope, so characteristic of man, can be found,' Schorger writes, 'than the search for a living wild passenger pigeon long after it had ceased to exist.'[13] Federal and state wildlife-protection laws were passed, too late for the passenger pigeon but in time to save animals such as the American bison, another once-plentiful species that had been pushed to the verge of extinction.

On a psychological level, people struggled with the knowledge that extinction could happen so quickly and that we could be the cause. It suggested a profoundly disquieting thought: if an apparently successful species like the passenger pigeon could go extinct, couldn't the same thing happen to us?

In 1947, the Wisconsin Society for Ornithology erected a monument to the passenger pigeon in Wyalusing State Park, near the site of the great nesting of 1871, with this inscription: 'This species became extinct through the avarice and thoughtlessness of man.' Like most epitaphs, it's a teaser. It hints at what happened but leaves a lot unsaid. What was the relation between 'avarice' and 'thoughtlessness' – did avarice overwhelm thought, or did thoughtlessness leave the door open to avarice? What thought or thoughts, exactly, were missing? And did the blame lie with 'man' or with particular men?

A recurrent theme in the narratives of American environmentalism is that people are bad. Humans, in this telling, are sinners, a cancerous growth on the face of the planet. The traditional goal of the environmental movement has been to restore a baseline, a state of nature that existed before human defilement. But however well these people-versus-nature narratives served environmentalism over the past century, the time has come to dismantle them and erect a new intellectual scaffolding.

Monument to the now-extinct passenger pigeon in Wisconsin's Wyalusing State Park. *Photo: Wisconsin Historical Society, WHS-34683.*

Just as the passenger pigeon's demise helped to shape twentieth-century environmentalism, so might a new and unlikely effort to resurrect the species change environmental thought and practice in the coming century. In February 2012, an invitation-only meeting was hosted at Harvard Medical School by George Church, a pioneer of genetic sequencing and the leader of the synthetic-biology team at Harvard's Wyss Institute for Biologically Inspired Engineering. It was convened by Stewart Brand, who heads the Long Now Foundation in San Francisco, and his wife, Ryan Phelan, the founder and former CEO of a genetic-testing company called DNA Direct. The meeting's purpose was to consider using recent advances in genetic engineering to bring back the passenger pigeon.

The idea originally came from Brand, who was the founding editor of the *Whole Earth Catalog*. In an email to Church and the Harvard biologist Edward O. Wilson, he wrote, 'The death of the last passenger pigeon in 1914 was an event that broke the public's heart and persuaded everyone that extinction is the core of humanity's relation with nature.' He asked Church, who had already raised the possibility of bringing back the woolly mammoth, whether it would be possible to recreate the passenger pigeon. Brand seemed motivated less by the passenger pigeon's importance to the environment than by its importance to environmental ideology. 'The environmental and conservation movements have mired themselves in a tragic view of life,' he explained. 'The return of the passenger pigeon could shake them out of it – and invite them to embrace prudent biotechnology as a Green tool instead of a menace in this century.'[14]

According to the *New York Times Magazine*, Church wrote back within three hours with 'a detailed plan to return "a flock of millions to billions" of passenger pigeons to the planet'. The plan proposed extracting DNA fragments from museum specimens of passenger-pigeon remains and combining these with DNA from the bird's closest living relative, the band-tailed pigeon. Germ cells with the new genome would be inserted into the eggs of band-tailed pigeons, and the resulting chicks should produce offspring that carry traits from both species. The progeny would then be crossed through several generations to breed a new species that, while not identical to the original, would come pretty close.[15] Brand and Phelan founded an outfit called Revive and Restore, with Phelan as its executive director, to translate the concept into reality.

Not everyone is convinced that this is a great idea. David Blockstein, a passenger-pigeon expert and senior scientist at the National Council for Science and the Environment, who participated in the Harvard meeting, is among the skeptics. 'Suppose you did create a pseudo–passenger pigeon. Then what?' he asks. 'This was a bird that needed hundreds of thousands of other birds to survive. How do you get there?'[16] Blockstein also worries that efforts to revive extinct species could divert scarce resources from efforts to save endangered species that still exist, and that our commitment to saving them could be undermined if we come to believe that extinction is something we can reverse whenever we want. (It's also much cheaper to keep a species alive than it is to resurrect it.)

Others have been more receptive. In March 2013 the National Geographic Society hosted a TEDx conference on 'de-extinction' at its Washington headquarters that was convened by Revive and Restore. It featured discussions about efforts to bring back the passenger pigeon, the woolly mammoth, the Tasmanian tiger and other species. Two months later, *Audubon* magazine carried a short interview with Ben Novak, a researcher at Revive and Restore, under the cheery headline 'Welcome Back'. The public appears to like the idea of de-extinction, or at least to accept it as possible and hence probably inevitable, influenced perhaps by *Jurassic Park*. The *Times Magazine*, citing a Pew poll from 2010, noted that 'belief in de-extinction trails belief in evolution by only 10 percentage points'.

Restoring the passenger pigeon, or a facsimile of it, could mark a turning point in the attitudes of environmentalists toward new biotechnologies, in part by challenging the people-are-bad narrative. But de-extinction perpetuates another dubious tenet of environmental ideology, one that coalesced a century ago: the idea that it's always preferable to return to a bygone baseline. For better or worse, ecosystems change. A big question – the mammoth in the room – is what's better and what's worse. It's not obvious that turning back the clock is necessarily a good idea when the clock has kept ticking.

In thinking about what we should and should not do to create better ecosystems, history suggests that a certain degree of humility is in order. In 1872, a Cincinnati businessman named Andrew Erkenbrecher founded the Society for the Acclimatization of Birds, with the aim of importing non-native bird species from Europe to combat a local caterpillar infestation. (The next year he founded the Cincinnati Zoo, where Martha died.) Among the species Erkenbrecher introduced to Cincinnati was the common starling. Although his first introductions did not survive, subsequent starling releases successfully established the species that Edward O. Wilson has called 'a plague across America'.[17] The worldwide starling population today is estimated at 600 million, about one-third of which are in the Western Hemisphere. If we bring back passenger pigeons in even greater numbers, it's not evident that this will be counted as a blessing a century from now.

Rather than pursue the hope that we can reverse time and retrieve a happy ending, perhaps we need to learn to admit it when we make terrible mistakes, absorb their lessons and move on.

When I visited Robert Askins, a Connecticut College ornithologist and the author of *Restoring North America's Birds*, he recalled the condition of bird populations at the close of the nineteenth century. The picture he painted was bleak. 'After the passenger pigeon, the market hunters didn't go into some other line of work,' he said. 'They just moved on to other species. Back in 1900 you would have seen few water birds around here. No egrets. No sandpipers. Any ducks that survived would have been so gun-shy that you wouldn't know they were there.'

Much has changed since then, and from the standpoint of wild birds, it's not all bad. The Migratory Bird Treaty Act of 1918 banned the hunting and sale of most bird species. Thanks to the growth of the domesticated poultry industry, Americans eat more bird meat but a lot less wild fowl. In the middle of the century, when a new threat to birds emerged from DDT and similar pesticides, Rachel Carson's *Silent Spring* helped to inspire a ban on their use. Concerted and even heroic efforts were undertaken to restore populations of threatened species like the bald eagle and the wild turkey.

This does not mean that everything is hunky-dory. Climate change now threatens birds and all other living things. Birds may initially fare better than other species by virtue of their mobility. (In New England, where I live, southern species like the cardinal, the tufted titmouse and the Carolina wren have become common residents.) But the ecosystems on which they rely for food cannot move as quickly. The environmental challenges we face today differ from those we faced a century ago. Our narratives must change, too. New technologies – notably, energy technologies – will be necessary part of any solution. The quest to preserve or restore a baseline state of nature, always a mirage, is slowly being abandoned; ecologists have begun to think in terms of maintaining valuable processes rather than trying to freeze the biological landscape.

Humans are part of the web of life, and we can – and sometimes do – have positive impacts on the rest of nature. The old, people-are-bad, nature-is-good formula, which was so central to the environmentalism that was born when Martha died, is too glib and all too often counterproductive. It is time to fashion a new environmentalism, an environmentalism founded on definitions of good and bad that do not estrange humankind from nature.

Part II
ENVIRONMENTAL INJUSTICE

Chapter 9

INEQUALITY AND THE ENVIRONMENT*

Inequality in the distribution of wealth and power is both a cause and a consequence of environmental degradation.

Inequality as a Cause of Environmental Degradation

I began my career in the field of agricultural development. In the middle of my undergraduate studies I worked for two years in the Indian state of Bihar on a Gandhian land-reform project. A few years later, my partner Betsy Hartmann and I lived in a Bangladesh village with the aim of writing a book to address some basic questions that Westerners have about people in what used to be called the Third World. Questions like: What are the causes of poverty and hunger? What is the position of women? What's the role of religion? What's the impact of foreign aid? In our book, *A Quiet Violence*, we explored these issues through the stories of real people, as much as possible in their own words.[1]

For me these were formative experiences. Living with some of the world's poorest people, and coming to see life through their eyes, profoundly shaped my understanding of the world and its problems. One of the most important lessons was about the debilitating effects of the unequal distribution of wealth and power. I came to understand the simple fact that the reason why hundreds of millions of people around the world went hungry, then and still today, is not because there's not enough food but because they lack the purchasing power to buy it in the market and the political power to obtain it by other means. The peasant farmers and agricultural labourers of Bangladesh and Bihar understood this clearly, even though it came as news to many economists a few years later when Amartya Sen published his landmark book, *Poverty and Famines*.[2]

* Lecture delivered at Tufts University, March 2017, on receiving the Leontief Prize for Advancing the Frontiers of Economic Thought.

In South Asia I also began to recognize that inequality not only determines who eats and who starves, with results that can be tragic and obscene, but also constrains productivity, resulting a smaller economic pie than would exist in a more egalitarian and productive society – a result that can be termed the 'inefficiency of inequality'.

When I entered graduate school at Oxford, a decade after having first set foot in Bihar, this was the topic I wanted to explore. At Oxford I was fortunate to study with two brilliant economists, Keith Griffin and Amartya Sen. With their guidance I returned to South Asia to carry out research for my dissertation, which analysed how agrarian inequalities impede the development of irrigation and water control to the detriment of rice production. This became my book *Agrarian Impasse in Bengal*.[3]

I mention this background here because the human relationship to the environment – as a source of raw materials and as a sink for disposal of wastes – is similar in important ways to the relationship that South Asian villagers have to the land. In both cases, the distribution of wealth and power determines who gets what, and also shapes how we use – or abuse – nature's wealth.

After completing my doctorate, I accepted a job in the University of Massachusetts (UMass) Amherst economics department – then, as now, an oasis for free thought in a discipline that too often seems to believe in a free market in everything but ideas. The intellectual blinders on economists were particularly tight at that time, the era of Ronald Reagan and Margaret Thatcher. At UMass I started a course called 'The Political Economy of the Environment' in which my students and I explored interactions between inequality and the environment.

In the early 1990s, I received a Fulbright fellowship to go to Costa Rica to help establish a master's programme in ecological economics and sustainable development at the National University. While there I was invited to speak at a conference – it was my first public presentation in Spanish – on political economy and the environment.

The English version of that talk appeared in the journal *Ecological Economics* in 1994. It was titled 'Inequality as a Cause of Environmental Degradation'. This was an effort to theorize how the inequalities of power and wealth that structure our relationships with each other also structure our relationships with nature. I began by observing that wherever we encounter environmental degradation, we can pose three basic questions:

- First, who benefits from the activities that cause the problem? If nobody wins – or, at least, thinks they'll win – the activities would not occur.
- Second, who bears the cost? If no one were harmed by these activities, there wouldn't be a problem – at least from the standpoint of human welfare.
- Third, why is it that the winners are able to impose these costs on the losers?

I suggested three possible answers to this last question. One is that those who will lose do not yet exist: they belong to future generations who are not here to defend themselves. In such cases, the only solution is for the present generation to cultivate an ethic of responsibility towards those who will follow us, an ethic that in my mind goes together with a sense of gratitude for what we have received from those who came before.

The second possibility is that those who bear environmental costs lack information. They may know that their children are getting sick but not that the cause is pollution from a nearby factory. In such cases, the solution lies in environmental education – including, crucially, the right to know what is in our environment and who put it there.

The third possibility is that those who are being harmed are here today, and are well aware of what's happening, but that they lack sufficient wealth and power to prevail against those who benefit from the environmentally degrading activities. I called this the 'power-weighted social decision rule': a society's decisions about whether, when and where to degrade (or protect) the environment are shaped by the preferences and relative power of those who win and lose from that decision.

The power to influence environmental outcomes operates in both the market and in the state. In the sphere of the market we call it 'purchasing power'. In the sphere of the state we call it 'political power'. These two domains of power are correlated: people with more wealth tend to have more political influence, and vice versa.

The state-market dichotomy dominated political and economic discourse in the nineteenth and twentieth centuries, demarcating 'left' from 'right'. But in analysing the political economy of environmental degradation we can discern a more fundamental dichotomy: between societies with democratic versus oligarchic distributions of wealth and power.

I hypothesized in my 1994 paper that wider inequalities of wealth and power generally result in more environmental degradation. At the time, this was a decidedly unpopular view. A referee for a volume to which I was invited to contribute a follow-up paper panned the idea, asserting that 'Boyce is beating a dead horse', a phrase that for some reason stuck in my mind. I think he meant that in the end-of-history days of the roaring nineties, no one still believed that inequality was something to get worked up about.

It turns out the horse was only on tranquilizers. Now it's wide awake and kicking, and today inequality is all the rage – in more senses than one.

Subsequent research has tested the power-weighted social decision rule hypothesis against empirical evidence. Analysing international variations in pollution and other environmental indicators, Mariano Torras and I found that equality – especially when measured by the extent of literacy and political rights and civil liberties – is a strong predictor of environmental degradation.[4] Similarly, when several colleagues and I analysed interstate variations in the United States, we found that states with a more equal distribution of power – as proxied by voter participation, educational attainment and fiscal policy fairness – tend to have stronger environmental policies, better environmental outcomes and, as a result, better public health.[5]

Returning to South Asia for a moment, the Indian scholar Bina Agarwal has documented the environmental impacts of inequality along the axis of gender. In India's forest-dependent communities, those where women participate in management committees generally use forest resources more sustainably than those where women are excluded.[6] Gender equity is not only good for women – it turns out to be good for the environment, too.

More research remains to be done to understand how inequality affects the environment.[7] But it is no longer outlandish to maintain that it does.

Environmental Degradation as a Cause of Inequality

Let us now turn to causal linkages in the reverse direction, running from environmental degradation to inequality.

Another hypothesis suggested by the power-weighted social decision rule is that environmental costs are not distributed randomly across the population. They are not impartial 'externalities'. Instead these costs are imposed disproportionately on communities with less wealth and power.

This prediction is consistent with the findings of the now-extensive literature on environmental justice (EJ). Beginning in the 1980s, Robert Bullard and other researchers began to document systematic disparities in exposure to environmental hazards in the United States, focusing initially on the disproportionate siting of toxic waste dumps in African American neighbourhoods.[8] These findings, coupled with pressure from EJ activists, led to President Clinton's 1994 executive order directing federal agencies to identify and address disproportionately high and adverse human health and environmental impacts on minorities and low-income populations.

Since then, EJ researchers have produced an extensive body of evidence documenting the fact that environmental disparities mirror inequalities in the distribution of wealth and power.[9] A notable finding in this literature is that race and ethnicity are highly significant predictors of environmental harm, even after controlling for the effect of income. This casts doubt on the claim that market dynamics, arising from lower housing prices in more polluted neighbourhoods, suffice to explain environmental disparities. It attests instead to the enduring connections between race and power in America – political power as well as purchasing power.

Indeed, there is evidence that in the United States environmental inequalities are wider than income inequalities. Exposure to toxic air pollution from industrial sites, for example, is more unequally distributed than income, both vertically (from lowest to highest) and horizontally (between groups defined by race and ethnicity).[10]

In response to these findings, some might ask, 'So what?' By many measures – including life expectancy, income, employment, education and incarceration rates – there are vast inequalities in the United States, both vertical and horizontal. In this landscape of multiple and overlapping disparities, how important is the environmental layer?

Put differently, is environmental quality a luxury? Is it something that affluent and perhaps middle-class people can afford to worry about, but that ranks low on the list of priorities for disadvantaged communities?

Apart from its intrinsic value as a basic human right, a clean and safe environment has important instrumental value, too, particularly for children. For example, when Manuel Pastor and his colleagues analysed school performance in Los Angeles, controlling for usual determinants such as parental income and education, class size and teacher salaries, they discovered that exposure to air toxics has a significant negative effect on standardized test scores.[11] Pollution exposure has serious adverse impacts on fetal and child health.[12] It also results in lower property values, more days lost from work due to illness and caring for sick kids, and higher healthcare expenditures.[13]

Low-income and minority communities across the country have given their own answer to the 'so what' question by mobilizing to fight against contamination of their air and water. Indeed, polls in the United States find that people of colour often are more environmentally aware than whites. An ABC News/Washington Post poll released in November 2015, for example, found that 78 per cent of non-whites agreed with the statement that climate change is a serious problem, compared to 56 per cent of whites.[14]

A final important point about EJ is that it is not a zero-sum game. At first blush, one might imagine that higher pollution burdens for people of color mean a cleaner environment for Anglo whites. But the total quantity of pollution varies across locations, as well as its distribution. It turns out that places where industrial air pollution is more unequally distributed tend to have higher exposure for everyone, including whites.[15] Perhaps corporations act as if the cost of pollution is lower when it's borne primarily by minorities, so they emit more of it. Perhaps whites expend more political capital to influence zoning and housing policies in regions with higher pollution. Or perhaps – a dispiriting thought – whites care more about their pollution burden relative to minorities than they do about its absolute level. Whatever the reasons, this pattern implies that EJ can be good for white folks, too.

Policies to Combat Inequality and Environmental Degradation

I was given the opportunity to work more on the policy implications of the links between inequality and the environment starting in the late 1990s, when my colleagues Robert Pollin and Gerald Epstein established the Political Economy Research Institute (PERI) at UMass Amherst. PERI provided a platform for me to launch a number of collaborative research projects.

One of these was the Natural Assets Project. This was the brainchild of Michael Conroy, who at the time was working as a programme officer at the Ford Foundation. Its aim was to explore how environmental protection can be reframed as building assets in the hands of low-income communities and individuals. The project gave me the opportunity to bring together a remarkable group of scholars and activists from around the country and around the world, and I learned a great deal from them. I will conclude with two examples of the natural asset-building strategies that we proposed.[16]

Cultivated biodiversity

The first is a strategy for conservation of the biodiversity that underpins long-term food security for humankind. I am referring here to genetic diversity in crops and livestock, the cultivated biodiversity that evolved through what Charles Darwin, in the opening chapter of *On the Origin of Species*, called 'artificial selection'.[17]

Artificial selection is the evolutionary process, guided through millennia by human hands, by which plants and animals were first domesticated and then diversified into thousands of distinct varieties adapted to environmental and cultural differences across the globe. This diversity provides the foundation for the ability of agriculture – 'modern' as well as 'traditional' – to adapt to changing pest and pathogen populations, and also, in coming years, to climate change.

A hallmark of industrial agriculture has been the displacement of these diverse varieties by a handful that have been bred to maximize specific properties, above all the ability to turn fertilizer into grain. The resulting crop monocultures may be 'efficient' from the perspective of short-run profit maximization, but they achieve this at the long-run peril of putting all our eggs in one basket. To adapt to changing environmental conditions over time, agriculture depends on the suite of diverse varieties that is being eroded by modern agriculture itself.

This genetic erosion ranks alongside climate change as perhaps the greatest environmental challenge of our time. Regrettably, it does not receive commensurate public attention, perhaps in part because many environmentalists, especially in the United States, are wedded to a vision of 'wild' nature that disdains human-altered landscapes and cultivated biodiversity.

Fortunately, the loss of crop and livestock diversity remains far from complete. Across the world, and especially in the historic centres of origin of crops that as the great Russian biologist Nikolai Vavilov recognized are the modern centers of diversity, farmers carry on the long tradition of conservation and ongoing evolution of cultivated diversity. These farmers include *campesinos* growing maize and beans in the hills of south-central Mexico and Guatemala and potatoes in the Andes; peasants cultivating rice in south and southeast Asia; and small farmers tilling wheat and barley in the western and central Asia and millets in Africa.

Apart from cultivating diversity, what do these cultivators have in common? First, they are poor, often desperately so. Second, far from being appreciated for their vital contribution to current and future food security for humankind, they are looked down upon. They are scorned as backward by elites in their own countries and most international development experts, too. Third, their livelihoods today are being threatened by cheap imports from industrial agriculture that often are dumped below the market cost of production, let alone their environmental cost. Finally, as a result, more and more of them – particularly young people – are abandoning the land to seek a better life elsewhere. As they do so, the erosion of crop and livestock diversity accelerates.

It would be a mistake to think we can fully insure against this loss of biodiversity by simply storing specimens in 'gene banks'. *Ex situ*, off-site collections, like the one at the National Laboratory for Genetic Resources Preservation in Fort Collins, Colorado, are tremendously valuable, and it is vital that we fund them and keep them under public control. But they are not an adequate substitute for *in situ*, in-the-field diversity for three reasons.

First, gene banks can never be 100 per cent secure. Accidents happen. So do wars and natural disasters. Biological material is not inert, like gold and silver. Seeds must be stored under the right temperature and humidity, and periodically replanted, harvested and stored again – otherwise they die.

Second, simply having seeds in the bank does not mean we know what we have. The records may show that a packet of seeds was collected in a given time and place, but we don't know whether this variety is resistant to new strains of insects or diseases or climate variations. The farmers who grow them are the repositories of this knowledge, and without them the seeds lose much of their value.

Finally, even if gene banks were perfectly secure (which they are not) and we even if knew all there is to know about every variety (which we cannot), the most they can do is to freeze in place the existing stock of genetic diversity. Gene banks do not replicate the ongoing evolution of diversity in the field under the pressure of evolving pests, pathogens and climate changes. The interaction between humans and nature that originally created and now sustains this biodiversity cannot be stored in a vault.

The good news is that we can maintain diversity in the field by rewarding the farmers around the world who cultivate it. This will require a radical shift in agricultural policies, however. Instead of subsidizing industrial monocultures, we need to reallocate public resources and recognition to small farmers, above all in the centres of diversity. We need to abandon our myopic definition of 'efficiency' and replace it with a more robust standard that embraces resilience and sustainability. Rather than undermining the livelihoods of the women and men who cultivate diversity, we need to reward them. Rather than disparaging them, we should thank them. By rewarding their vital contributions to the common good, we can reduce inequality and help to protect the environment at the same time.

Carbon dividends

Let me turn lastly to the other great environmental challenge of our time, global climate change.

In one sense, just about anything we do to mitigate climate change will mitigate inequality, too, since it is the poorest people at home and abroad who are most vulnerable to the impacts of climate destabilization. This grim reality was illustrated vividly in New Orleans in 2005, when those who lost their homes and lives to Hurricane Katrina were disproportionately poor and disproportionately black.[18]

Burning fossil fuels releases a toxic stew of pollutants – including sulfur dioxide, nitrogen oxides and fine particulates – along with carbon dioxide, the main greenhouse gas. For this reason, curbing their use will generate air quality and public health 'co-benefits'. Because they bear the highest pollution burdens, low-income and disadvantaged communities stand to gain the most from cleaner air, especially if climate policies are designed with these benefits in mind.[19]

The clean energy transition will require very large investments in energy efficiency and renewables. As my PERI colleagues Bob Pollin and Heidi Garrett-Peltier have shown, these require considerably more labour per investment dollar than does fossil fuel extraction. Retrofitting buildings for energy efficiency, for example, creates many jobs in the building and construction trades. In economies with substantial unemployment and underemployment, these employment gains also can make a major contribution to the reduction of inequality.[20]

There is an additional way that climate policy can reduce inequality: carbon dividends. This is an idea I first learned about from Peter Barnes, a colleague in the Natural Assets Project.

One key element of effective climate policy is putting a price on carbon emissions. This can be done by means of either a carbon tax or a cap-and-permit system. From an administrative standpoint, it is simplest to charge the price where fossil carbon enters the economy, at the tanker port or coal-mine head or natural gas terminal. The tax or permit cost enters into the price of the fuel and is passed on to final users, including you and me. This provides an incentive for households, businesses and governments to consume less carbon and invest in energy efficiency and renewables.[21]

A drawback of carbon pricing – of any policy that increases fuel prices – is that it is distributionally regressive. Richer households typically have bigger carbon footprints than low-income and middle-class households, for the simple reason that they consume more of just about everything. In absolute dollar amounts they would pay more as a result of a carbon price. As a percentage of income, however, poor households would pay more than the rich, reflecting the fact that fuels are a necessity, not a luxury. On its own, therefore, carbon pricing would exacerbate economic inequality rather than reducing it.[22]

But the extra money that consumers pay as a result of carbon pricing does not evaporate. It is not shot to the moon or buried in the backyard. It is not sent to Saudi Arabia and other oil producers. Instead this money is available for recycling within the economy of the nation or state that charges the carbon price.

One way to recycle part or all of the money is through dividends that are paid equally to every resident. This has been proposed in the United States by Senators Maria Cantwell and Susan Collins, and by Congressman (now Senator) Chris Van Hollen. They have sponsored bills that would set a cap on carbon emissions that tightens over time, issue permits up to this limit, auction all the permits and return all or most of the revenue to the people as dividends.[23]

Carbon dividends are an example of a broader class of policies that would provide universal basic income from assets that we own in common.[24] For example, the state of Alaska pays equal dividends annually to all residents from its oil revenues.

Since carbon dividends would be paid equally to all, regardless of how much fossil fuel they personally use, everyone would still have a strong incentive to reduce their consumption of fossil fuels. Recycling carbon revenues as dividends changes the regressive impact of carbon pricing into a progressive net impact. Most low-income households would come out ahead in pocketbook terms, since the dividends would exceed their increased fuel costs. Middle-class households generally would break even, with the dividends protecting their real incomes. Most rich households would pay more than they get back in dividends, but they can afford it – and they and their children would share in the benefits of climate stabilization and clean air.

Much as rewarding small farmers for sustaining crop genetic diversity would combat inequality and protect our environment simultaneously, so would price-and-dividend carbon policies. As these examples illustrate, fighting inequality and fighting environmental degradation are not only complementary in theory. They can be pursued together in practice.

This is where I believe environmentalism is headed in the twenty-first century. We will not safeguard the environment without addressing the inequalities of wealth and power that perpetuate pollution and natural resource depletion. And we will not achieve a more equitable society without protecting our environment. I am grateful and honored to receive the Leontief Prize for my contributions to understanding the links between inequality and the environment. If my work helps others to make these connections and to act upon them, I will feel that I have done something to earn it.

Chapter 10

CLEAN AIR FOR ALL

Environmental justice is good for white folks, too.

Is environmental racism good for white folks? The answer isn't as obvious as it might seem.

In the United States, there is plenty of evidence that African Americans, Latinos, Asian Americans and Native Americans typically face greater pollution burdens than whites, with associated health risks.[1] So if the same total amount of pollution was spread more evenly, whites would wind up breathing dirtier air.

But would total pollution remain the same? Or would pollution decline if it was no longer disproportionately inflicted on minorities?

A study by a team of researchers at the University of Massachusetts Amherst finds that the quantity of toxic air pollution from industrial facilities is a variable, not a constant, and that the total pollution load is correlated with the extent to which minorities bear higher-than-average pollution impacts.[2]

Our team measured the extent of disparities in US metropolitan areas by comparing the share of minorities in total exposure risks from industrial air toxics, calculated from US Environmental Protection Agency data, to their share of metropolitan population. In Birmingham, Alabama, for example, minorities bear 62 per cent of the exposure risk but comprise only 31 per cent of the population.

In metropolitan areas that rank in the top 5 per cent nationwide in the difference between the share of exposure risk borne by minorities and their share of the population – what we call the 'minority discrepancy' – the average toxic exposure for all residents is more than double that in metropolitan areas that rank in the lower 75 per cent. In high-discrepancy cities, average exposure for minorities is almost four times more than in low-discrepancy cities, but for whites, too, average exposure is higher by a factor of about 60 per cent.

There are two main ways this striking correlation may be explained. One possibility is that wider discrepancies lead to more pollution. The perception that environmental costs can be shifted onto minorities may translate into

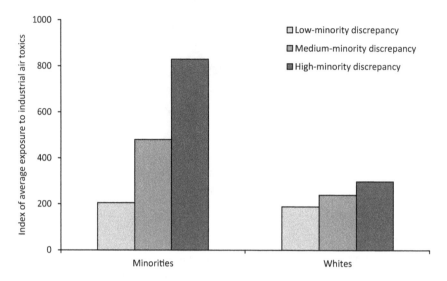

Figure 10.1 Exposure to toxic air pollution in US metropolitan areas

Exposure to toxic air pollution from industrial sources varies across the United States. In metropolitan areas with the widest exposure discrepancies between minorities and Anglo whites, all residents – whites as well as minorities – face higher pollution burdens than in metropolitan areas with low discrepancies.

weaker environmental regulation at existing facilities and greater willingness to accept new polluting facilities. If so, the fact that whites end up breathing dirtier air, too, implies that they do not fully escape the consequences.

A second possibility is that more pollution leads to wider discrepancies. Some cities may have high levels of industrial pollution for historical reasons, such as proximity to markets or inputs. In these places, whites may have invested more political capital in zoning and housing policies that shift pollution burdens onto minorities (see Figure 10.1).

Both explanations could contribute to the outcomes that we observe. In either case, the fact that minorities face heavier pollution burdens attests to the continuing importance of race and ethnicity in the distribution of political power in the United States.

Income matters for pollution exposure, too. Among both whites and minorities, households with incomes below the poverty line have higher-than-average exposure. But race and ethnicity have stronger effects than income. As a result, the average exposure faced by non-poor minorities is 20 per cent higher than it is for poor whites. This means that environmental disparities cannot be attributed simply to market forces, whereby pollution depresses property values and this induces poor people to move into the neighbourhood. Other forces are at work.

Environmental justice advocates firmly reject the charge that they are merely engaged in NIMBYism – the 'Not in My Back Yard' politics that seeks to displace hazards onto other communities. Instead, they voice the more inclusive demand, 'Not in Anyone's Back Yard'. These findings suggest that this is more than a slogan, and that advances in environmental justice could lead to cleaner air for all Americans, regardless of race, ethnicity or class.

Chapter 11

LETTER FROM FLINT

Flint, Michigan's transformation from industrial wonder to urban disaster shows the perils of elevating consumption above citizenship.

It began on 30 December 1936, at Fisher Body No. 1 in Flint, Michigan: workers occupied General Motors factories, launching one of the landmark struggles in US labour history. A Women's Emergency Brigade brought them food; when the police tried to drive out the strikers with tear gas, the women broke the windows to give them fresh air.[1] After 44 bitter winter days, the sit-down strike forced GM to recognize their union, the United Auto Workers.[2]

It was not an accident that Flint was the scene of this historic battle. One hundred years ago, when the city boasted the largest factory in the world – a Buick plant – the people of Flint elected a socialist mayor. But GM founding partner Charles S. Mott won two years later, campaigning on a platform whose first point was 'Only men who are successful at business should run city affairs.'

The US auto industry pioneered not only mass production but also mass consumption. 'The American citizen's first importance to his country is no longer that of citizen but that of consumer,' the pro-business *Flint Journal* editorialized in 1924. 'Consumption is the new necessity.'

By the early 1950s, when I was a baby and my parents moved there, Flint's workers were earning the highest industrial wages in the nation. In an exhibit called 'Flint and the American Dream', the city's Sloan Museum today displays the household belongings of a typical auto worker of that era: the kitchen appliances, formica countertops, chrome-and-vinyl furniture, the lawn mower and charcoal grill of my childhood.

Flint's American dream is now a distant memory. Starting in the 1970s, one auto plant after another shut down, a downward slide vividly portrayed in Michael Moore's 1989 film *Roger & Me*. In the 1981 recession, Flint had the highest unemployment rate in the country. Today, despite the fact that Flint's population has fallen to less than 60 per cent of what it was in 1960, the city's unemployment rate still ranks in the top 50 among the country's

The Flint sit-down strike of 1936–37 was a landmark struggle in the history of the US labor movement. After World War Two, Flint's auto workers had the highest industrial wages in the world. *Photo: Sloan Longway Museum.*

372 metropolitan areas. In the neighbourhood of company-built bungalows where I lived as a toddler, the pavements are cracked, the median strips are overgrown with weeds, and abandoned, burnt-out houses decay among the surviving homes.

How did this reversal of fortunes happen?

The reasons behind Flint's collapse are not only the greed and sheer ineptitude of GM's management, memorably depicted in *Roger & Me*, but also monumental public policy failures. These include the following:

- massive foreign borrowing, an overvalued dollar and unprecedented trade deficits, beginning in the Reagan era, the fatal macroeconomic nexus that decimated American manufacturing;
- the failure to grow Medicare into a nationwide single-payer healthcare system, leaving US firms – alone among those of advanced industrialized countries – saddled with employer-provided health insurance costs that further eroded their competitiveness;[3] and

Today Flint is among the poorest cities in the United States. Abandoned homes pockmark the author's old neighborhood. *Photo: James K. Boyce.*

- racial divisions, 'white flight' to the suburbs, and ill-conceived expressways that tore apart the social capital that was needed to mount an effective local response to these crises.

The grim result was that the American auto industry, which already had pioneered planned obsolescence in consumer goods, went a step further: Flint became a disposable city.

What can we learn from Flint's history? In hindsight, the consumption-based social contract espoused by the *Flint Journal* was not sustainable. It turns out that being a consumer is not a substitute for being a citizen. Caring about things is not more important than caring about each other. Private goodies are not a worthy substitute for public goods. Government cannot be entrusted safely to captains of industry. Our ability to consume cannot be detached from our responsibility to govern ourselves.

So Flint's American nightmare teaches us this: When we elevate consumption above citizenship, we imperil not only our democracy but, in the end, our economy, too.

Chapter 12

LET THEM DRINK POLLUTION?

The lead poisoning crisis in Flint is not just about drinking water. And it's not just about Flint.

The tragedy in Flint, Michigan, where residents have been poisoned by lead contamination, is not just about drinking water. And it's not just about Flint. It's about race and class, and the stark contradiction between the American dream of equal rights and opportunity for all and the American nightmare of metastasizing inequality of wealth and power.

The link between environmental quality and economic inequality was spelled out more than two decades ago in a memorandum signed by Lawrence Summers, then chief economist of the World Bank, excerpts of which appeared in the *Economist* under the provocative title, 'Let Them Eat Pollution'. Starting from the premise that the costs of pollution depend on 'the forgone earnings from increased morbidity and mortality', Summers concluded that 'the economic logic of dumping a load of toxic waste in the lowest-wage country is impeccable and we should face up to that'.[1]

A different logic is supposed to underpin US environmental policies. The Federal Water Pollution Control Act mandates that water quality standards should 'protect the public health' – period. Its aim, as former Environmental Protection Agency (EPA) administrator Douglas Costle put it, is 'protection of the health of all Americans'.[2] Under the law, clean water is a right, not something to be provided only insofar as justified by the purchasing power of the community in question.

Even when cost-benefit calculations are brought to bear on environmental policy, the EPA uses a single 'value of a statistical life' – currently around $9 million – for every person in the country, rather than differentiating across individuals on the basis of income or other attributes.[3]

In practice, however, the role of costs and benefits in shaping public policies often depends on power of those to whom they accrue.[4] When those on the receiving end are poor, their interests – and their lives – often count for less, much as the Summers memo recommended. And when they are racial and ethnic minorities, the political process often discounts their well-being even more.

So it was that Flint – a city with the second highest poverty rate in the nation (surpassed only by Youngstown, Ohio), where more than half of the population is African American – wound up with lead in its water supply up to 866 times the legal limit.[5] The levels in some residents' homes were high enough for the EPA to classify the water as 'toxic waste'.

The contamination was a result of budget-cutting measures imposed by the city's 'emergency manager', who was installed by Michigan governor Rick Snyder with the power to override the elected city council. To save money, the city's water supply was switched to the heavily polluted Flint River in 2014.[6] At the same time, officials stopped adding treatment to control corrosion in the system's old lead pipes.[7] When residents complained about the discolored and foul-smelling water coming out of their taps, and researchers found evidence of lead contamination, their concerns were brushed aside by state officials.[8]

Governor Snyder denies that environmental racism has anything to do with the plight of Flint's residents.[9] There are still some people who will tell you that Earth is flat, too.

In a lead editorial, the *New York Times* accused the governor of 'depraved indifference' toward Flint's residents.[10] But the roots of the crisis go deeper than the failings of individual politicians or officials. What we're seeing today in Flint is an outcome of depraved inequalities – inequalities that are corroding the body politic nationwide along with the water pipes in Flint.

Flint wasn't always like this. When I lived there as a kid in the early 1950s, its workers earned the highest industrial wages in the nation. The American dream was alive. But in the ensuing decades the city was ripped apart by macroeconomic policies that decimated America's manufacturing industries, the failure to construct a national health system to relieve employers of the soaring costs of private insurance, and the debilitating racial and fiscal politics of metropolitan segregation.

It is only a small step from the emergence of 'sacrifice zones' at the losing end of America's widening economic and political chasms to the systematic violation of the right to a clean environment that we see in Flint.[11] It is not enough to pass legislation to protect the public health of all Americans. Good laws that are not enforced are no more than good intentions. For a functioning government – even, it turns out, a functioning water system – we need a functioning democracy.

The poisoning of Flint is a symptom of this deeper inequality crisis that affects us all.

Chapter 13

LETTER FROM DELHI

The people of Delhi, India, young and old, rich and poor, are exposed to some of the world's worst air pollution. But not all are harmed equally, and not all are equally to blame.

Arriving in Delhi in January, at the height of the winter pollution season, you notice the air as soon as you step off the plane. A pungent smell with hints of burning rubber and diesel fumes assaults the nose and stings the eyes. On the highway into the city center, a digital screen shining through the smog displays the current level of suspended particulate matter. You don't need to understand the numbers to know it's bad.

Delhi has extensive parks, broad avenues, beautiful buildings and a vibrant culture. But casting a pall – quite literally – over it all is the worst air pollution of any major city in the world.

I lived in Delhi in spring 2015, accompanying my wife who had a research fellowship there. I brought along work to do on air pollution inequality in the United States. For the first week, we stayed in a guesthouse near the centre of town. One night I was awakened around 2:00 a.m. by the acrid smell of pollution. To get back to sleep, I had to slip on an N95 pollution mask (at the suggestion of a doctor friend, I'd brought some with us).

In the morning it struck me that it would be absurd to devote all my time in Delhi to working on US air pollution while ignoring the far higher levels around me. In an environmental twist on the spiritual maxim, 'be here now', I resolved to educate myself about Delhi's air pollution and investigate what can be done about it.

One of the most dangerous air pollutants is particulate matter. In Delhi it comes from multiple sources, including diesel trucks that are allowed to pass through the city in the middle of the night, rapidly growing numbers of passenger vehicles, coal-burning power plants and brick kilns that ring the city, construction debris and open burning of wastes.[1] Particulates are measured by an Air Quality Index (AQI). An AQI below 50 is considered 'good'. Anything above 300 is considered 'hazardous' and would trigger emergency health warnings in many countries.

An intrepid team of Beijing-based volunteers today assembles real-time data from air pollution monitors around the world and posts them on the website *aqicn.org*. In Delhi I soon fell into the habit of checking the data from our nearest location several times a day. This could be pretty alarming. When I checked on the morning of Valentine's Day, the AQI for particulates was 399. Overnight it had hit at 668, off the standard AQI chart. Sometimes it soared even higher.

A month before I arrived in Delhi, the Centre for Science and Environment, India's leading environmental advocacy organization, released the results of a study in which several residents were equipped with handheld devices to monitor air pollution levels as they went about their activities in the course of a typical day.[2] Some of their readings topped 1,000.

A 2014 World Health Organization report identified Delhi as having the highest average level of particulate air pollution among 1,600 major cities worldwide.[3] In the past two years, according to a recent report in the *Hindustan Times*, Beijing's air qualified as 'healthy' for just 58 out of 730 days. Delhi's air qualified for only seven.[4]

In the run-up to President Obama's three-day visit to Delhi in January 2015, a satirical website reported that US security agencies were flying in 20,000 gallons of clean air for him to breathe, the Secret Service having concluded that 'more than any terrorist strike, the Delhi air poses a serious security threat to POTUS'.[5] Extrapolating perhaps a bit too literally from health risk statistics, Bloomberg.com reported that the visit took six hours off the president's lifespan.[6]

Air Pollution as Environmental Injustice

Everyone in Delhi, young and old, rich and poor alike, is exposed to air pollution. But not all are exposed equally. A 2011 study in the scientific journal *Atmospheric Environment* found that Delhi's low-income households experienced significant adverse health effects from air pollution, whereas high-income households were not significantly affected. Part of the explanation may be that affluent households have access to air conditioning as well as better health and nutrition. The authors also found that low-income men in Delhi spend on average about seven hours a day outdoors, whereas at the top of the income scale the time spent outdoors is close to zero.[7] A study by Professor Amit Garg of the Indian Institute of Management examined the correlation between suspended particulates and socio-economic status, and concluded that exposure is generally higher in the city's low-income neighbourhoods.[8]

Health risks for children are especially acute as their developing brains, lungs and immune systems are vulnerable to air pollution. A study for the Government of India's Central Pollution Control Board that examined more than 11,000 Delhi school children in the early 2000s found that 43.5 per cent of them had reduced lung function, which was likely to be irreversible.[9] The lower the family's socio-economic status, the higher the percentage. The study made recommendations on everything from where new schools should be sited to when children should be allowed to play outside. But according to its principal researcher, 'absolutely nothing was followed up on'.[10] Since that time Delhi's air pollution has deteriorated further.

Some of the most extreme exposures are experienced by those who earn their livings on Delhi's arterial roads, including drivers of the three-wheeled auto-rickshaws that ply the streets. A study of in-rickshaw pollution concentrations found that levels of ultra-fine particles were eight times higher than the levels at rooftop monitors one kilometre away.[11]

Just as not everyone is harmed equally by pollution, not everyone benefits equally from the activities that cause it. Delhi's upper-income residents 'consume more of energy intensive and emission-producing goods such as electricity and private transport', Garg observes, 'while the poor bear a dispro-portionately higher share of the resultant air pollution health burden'.

In other words, Delhi's air pollution is a classic case of environmental injustice. The distribution of its costs and benefits mirrors the distribution of wealth and power.

What to Do?

Public awareness of air pollution in Delhi lags behind that in China, where face masks are a common sight and the remarkable film *Under the Dome* received 100 million views within 48 hours when it was posted in March 2015 (before being banned by Chinese authorities).[12] But this may be starting to change. In spring 2015, the *Indian Express*, one of the country's leading newspapers, ran a searching multi-part investigative series on Delhi's air pollution called 'Death by Breath'.[13] The Centre of Science and Environment, which successfully campaigned a decade ago for conversion of Delhi's buses and autorickshaws from diesel to compressed natural gas, continues to raise public consciousness and advocates for policy remedies.

In the expatriate community, Delhi's toxic air is viewed with rising alarm. In 2014, the US embassy imported 1,800 top-of-the-line air purifiers for its personnel. 'My business has just taken off,' the director of a local firm selling air filtration units told the *New York Times*. 'It started in the diplomatic commu-nity, but it's spread to the high-level Indian community, too.'[14]

But such individual solutions – for the few who can afford them – can only go so far. Returning to the United States after three years as the *New York Times* Delhi correspondent, Gardiner Harris wrote that the city's air pollution is 'so frightening that some feel it is unethical for those who have a choice to willingly raise children here'. His own eight-year-old son suffered asthma attacks requiring emergency hospitalization. So many expatriates are leaving Delhi, he reported, that the American Embassy School is 'facing a steep drop in admissions next fall'.[15]

Indian government officials aspire to make Delhi a 'world-class city'.[16] This goal is utterly incompatible with the city's current air quality.

Because Delhi's pollution has multiple causes, clearing the air will require multiple solutions. Important measures that could be undertaken immediately include expanded pollution monitoring with real-time reporting of the results; emergency health advisories and school closings when pollution exceeds dangerous thresholds; and the provision of particulate-grade masks to autorickshaw drivers, traffic policemen and others who earn their livings on the streets, not only to protect them but also to build public awareness of the issue.

In the longer term, key measures in the transportation sector include cleaner fuel standards and a phase-out of diesel vehicles; completion of bypass roads, so long-distance trucks no longer pass through the city; the expansion of public transport, including state-of-the-art bus rapid transit systems plus pedestrian walkways and bicycle lanes for 'last-mile connectivity' between stops and final destinations; and a cap on numbers of private automobiles.

Other necessary measures include strict (and strictly enforced) controls on emissions from coal-fired power plants and brick kilns (and enforcement of the ban on burning old tires in the latter); a rapid buildout of clean, renewable electricity generation; and a ban on open burning of wastes, including the burning of plant debris and crop residues which effectively turns beneficial fertilizer into hazardous pollution.

These same measures would also reduce carbon dioxide emissions, helping to mitigate global climate change – a linkage that may help to unlock international finance for green infrastructure investments. The potential air quality co-benefits from curbing use of fossil fuels are substantial even in high-income countries with relatively clean air. In India, the public health co-benefits of a clean energy transition would be enormous.

Another possible source of finance would be revenues from capping the supply of automobile license plates and auctioning them to the highest bidder. In Singapore, which has been doing this since 1990, a license plate that is valid for 10 years costs US$60,000. The environmental writer Aseem Shrivastava and I have suggested a similar policy for Delhi with part of the auction revenue dedicated to green infrastructure and part returned to the residents of Delhi as equal dividend payments, based on the principle that the limited amount of public space that is available for private vehicles belongs in common measure to all the city's residents.[17]

Other major cities around the world have shown that clean air and economic development are not only compatible but can go together. These goals can be reconciled in Delhi, too, if and when its citizens demand it and its politicians respond.

Chapter 14

MAPPING THE ENVIRONMENTAL RISKSCAPE*

African Americans, Latinos and low-income communities bear outsized pollution burdens in the United States.

America's corporate polluters are not colour-blind. Nor are they oblivious to distinctions of class. Studies of environmental inequality have shown that minorities and low-income communities often bear disproportionate pollution burdens.[1] In other words, rather than being an impersonal 'externality' randomly distributed across the population, the distribution of pollution mirrors the distribution of power and wealth.

These disparities result from decisions by firms to site hazardous facilities in the most vulnerable communities and from decisions by government regulators to put lower priority on environmental enforcement in these communities. To some extent, they also may reflect demographic changes as pollution leads affluent people to move out, neighbourhood property values to fall and poorer households to move in. Even after controlling for income differences, however, racial and ethnic minorities typically face higher pollution burdens, a finding that implies that disparities are a result of differences in political power as well as purchasing power.

But the United States is a big country, and it is not homogeneous. Electoral politics, social movements, industrial structure, residential segregation and even laws and regulations differ greatly across the regions. The extent and pattern of environmental inequalities may vary, too.

In a recent study, we examined regional variations to tackle two key questions.[2] First, is minority status or income more important in explaining environmental disparities? Second, is higher income equally protective for whites and minorities in affecting pollution exposure?

---

* Co-authored with Klara Zwickl and Michael Ash.

In our study we used the US Environmental Protection Agency (EPA) database called Risk-Screening Environmental Indicators (RSEI). These data can be traced to the demands of environmental advocates for disclosure of information on the hazards faced by communities in the wake of the tragic 1984 accident at a chemical plant owned by a US company in Bhopal, India, in which thousands of nearby residents died and many more were severely injured. In response to this man-made disaster, the US Congress passed the Emergency Planning and Community Right-to-Know Act, which requires companies to report their releases of dangerous chemicals into our air, water and lands. The EPA makes this information available to the public in its annual Toxics Release Inventory. The RSEI database uses this information to estimate industrial pollution exposures in neighbourhoods throughout the country.

We merged RSEI air pollution data with census data on race, ethnicity and income in urban areas. The highest median exposures, as well as the highest 90th percentiles of exposure, occur in the Midwest, South Central and mid-Atlantic regions. In an econometric analysis that controls for intercity variations to identify disparities within cities, we found significant differences in exposure by both income and race/ethnicity nationwide and in most of the EPA regions.

Figure 14.1 shows how average exposure in these top three regions varies among four groups: non-poor whites, poor whites, non-poor minorities and poor minorities. Low income is a strong predictor of toxic risk: in all three regions, poor minorities face higher average exposure than non-poor minorities, and poor whites face higher exposure than non-poor whites. Minority status is a strong predictor, too: in fact, in the Midwest and South Central regions, non-poor minorities face higher exposure than poor whites. In the mid-Atlantic region, however, whites face higher exposure than minorities, a finding that points to important interregional variations in mapping the pollution riskscape.

Figure 14.2 shows how, at the national level, average exposures for African Americans and whites vary across neighbourhoods that have differing median incomes. Racial disparities in pollution exposure are wide among people living in low-income neighbourhoods. Among those living in the nation's poorest neighbourhoods, with median household incomes below $15,000/year, the average exposure of African Americans is 47 per cent higher than that of whites. The racial disparity shrinks as incomes rise. Beyond $25,000/year, neighbourhood incomes become more important than race as a predictor of pollution exposure.

More than half of African Americans live in neighbourhoods with median incomes below $25,000/year, compared to fewer than 12 per cent of whites.[3]

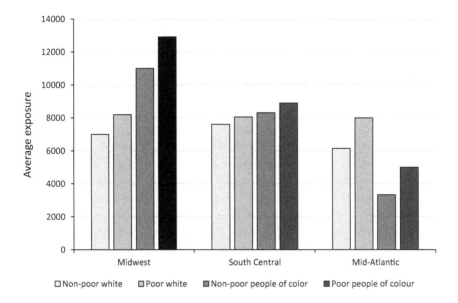

Figure 14.1 Average exposure by income and minority status

In the two regions most heavily polluted by industrial air toxics, the Midwest and South Central states, race trumps income as a predictor of exposure: *non-poor* minorities have higher average exposure than poor whites. In the mid-Atlantic region, whites have higher average exposure than minorities, but in both groups poor households have higher exposure than non-poor households.

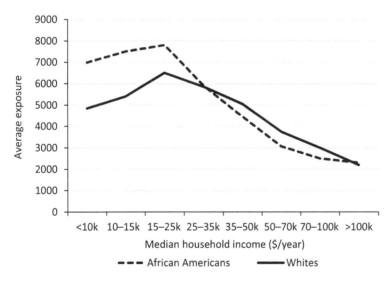

Figure 14.2 Average exposure by race and income in the United States

Among people living in neighbourhoods with median household incomes below $25,000/year, race is a stronger predictor of pollution exposure than income. In neighbourhoods with incomes above this level, median household income is a stronger predictor than race. Most African Americans live in the former; most whites live in the latter. It would not be surprising, therefore, if they view the relative importance of race and income differently.

We can conclude, therefore, that based on where they live, most whites are more likely to see income as the main factor explaining disparities in pollution exposure, while for most African Americans the racial composition of neighbourhoods appears to matter more.

These data provide important insights into relationships among race and ethnicity, class and pollution exposure in the United States. At the same time, much remains to be learned. Despite the successes of the environmental right-to-know movement, there are still many blind spots in our information about pollution exposure. For example, fracking wells for oil and natural gas extraction currently are exempt from the reporting requirements of the Emergency Planning and Community Right-to-Know Act. Other important environmental databases, such as the National Air Toxics Assessment, have not been updated for almost a decade. These gaps not only impede analysis of environmental injustice but also leave communities uncertain about environmental conditions in their neighbourhoods. Vigilance and advocacy are crucial to defend and extend the public's right to know about pollution and to make the right to a clean and safe environment a reality for all.

Chapter 15

MEASURING POLLUTION INEQUALITY

Air pollution in the United States is distributed even more unequally than income: an interview with Lynn Parramore of AlterNet.

Lynn Parramore (LP): Why did you decide to look at industrial air pollution and inequality? Why is this research important?

James Boyce (JB): What we wanted to do was look at inequalities in the environmental conditions that people experience here in the United States. Industrial air pollution is just one piece of a much broader set of environmental conditions. In addition to air pollution, for example, there's water pollution. And in addition to air pollution from industrial point sources, there's air pollution from mobile sources like cars and diesel trucks. So what we focused on was really one piece of a larger canvas of differences in pollution exposure across the population in this country.

There were two reasons we chose industrial air pollution to illustrate these disparities. One is that for the communities that are impacted by this sort of pollution, it's a very important piece of their total pollution burden. So it's not that it's the most important piece nationwide, but for communities with particularly high pollution burdens, it's a big deal.

The second reason is that the Environmental Protection Agency (EPA) has developed some very high-quality data on air pollution from these facilities. Back in the mid-1980s there was a terrible disaster at a plant owned by a US corporation called Union Carbide in the city of Bhopal in central India. In response to public concern about whether there might be similar risks at industrial facilities here in the United States, Congress passed legislation called the Emergency Planning and Community Right-to-Know-Act. This created something called the Toxics Release Inventory (TRI), which requires any facility in the United States that meets certain criteria to report to the EPA every year its releases of hundreds of toxic chemicals to the air, water and land. So it provides a really detailed database on emissions from industrial facilities.

In the 1990s, the EPA added some additional important pieces to the TRI data. The first is information on the relative toxicities of the chemicals. When inhaled, some of them, for example, pound per pound are 10 million times more toxic than other chemicals. The EPA also looked at how they're distributed in the environment. They modelled the plumes of exposure that result from these releases to see at a very fine level of geographical resolution what concentrations of different toxic chemicals were expected to be in the air as a result of releases. Then they ranked facilities in terms of the total public health hazards they posed. That was done in order to prioritize enforcement actions by the EPA and by the state environmental agencies. The tool that EPA created is called the Risk-Screening Environmental Indicators. That ranking of facilities is publicly available.

In our research, we've disaggregated the impact from each facility to be able to understand which communities are impacted and by how much. Among the things we can do is estimate – again, at a very fine level of geographical resolution – how much air pollution exposure there is from all the surrounding industrial facilities that are included in this EPA database. That gives us a way to look at how unequally air pollution from industrial facilities is distributed across the American landscape.

LP: What new information is presented in this paper? [1]

JB: We've been working with these data for several years now in a collaborative research project with researchers from the University of Michigan, the University of Southern California, and other institutions, and we've done a variety of studies that look, in particular, at patterns of environmental injustice in the US that result in disproportionate exposure of people of color and low-income communities.

What's new about this paper is that we developed three different inequality measures and applied these at the levels of individual states and the 435 Congressional districts in order to get a sense of how unequally exposure to industrial air toxins is distributed in these jurisdictions. To the best of my knowledge, no one has done that before.

In addition to looking at the ratios of exposures of people of colour versus whites and of people living below the federal poverty line versus the non-poor, we also developed an environmental version of the Gini coefficient, which ranks the population, in this case from the people with the dirtiest air to the people with the cleanest air, and measures how unequally air quality is distributed across the population in the states and Congressional districts. That was a new contribution.

LP: What stood out to you in the results?

JB: One of the take-home findings is that if you look at how unequally environmental quality is distributed in the US, it makes the inequality in the distribution of income look relatively modest. I wasn't entirely surprised to find that air quality is distributed even more unequally than income, but I was surprised at the magnitude of the difference. It's really striking.

Another thing that became clear is that how you measure inequality can have rather dramatic results on which communities stand out as being the most unequal. I was a bit surprised that states that ranked highest in terms of disproportionate exposures of racial and ethnic minorities, for example, did not necessarily rank highest in terms of overall disparities between the most exposed and the least exposed communities.

So from a methodological standpoint, I think our paper makes an important contribution in two ways. One is in showing that it's possible to measure inequality in the distribution of environmental quality, much as we measure inequality in the distribution of income and wealth. The second is to show that how different places rank in terms of environmental inequality depends on what specific measures of environmental inequality one is interested in.

If one is primarily interested in disparities in terms of race or ethnicity, then one can directly compare the measures that are relevant. If one is most interested in the extent of divergence between the most polluted and the least polluted communities, then a different measure is appropriate. Our study shows both that it's possible to look at these things and that in doing so we need to be sensitive to the measures we employ.

LP: How can a person of colour avoid air pollution? Do patterns of inequality differ across the country?

JB: Avoiding industrial air pollution is difficult, particularly if you're poor or a member of a racial or ethnic minority. That's partly because of housing prices. It's partly because of discrimination in housing and mortgage markets – the phenomenon of red-lining. And it's also partly because of the tendency for firms to site polluting facilities in relatively low-income and relatively high-minority communities because they expect less political pushback.

Rather than thinking about trying to move somewhere else to escape this, which is an attempt to find an individual solution to the problem, what folks really need to do – and are doing – is to join together with other members of their communities and press the polluters and the regulators to reduce the exposures that result from the activities of industrial facilities near them.

That's what the environmental justice (EJ) movement in the United States has been trying to do since its beginnings in the 1980s. There is still much that needs to be done, but the EJ movement has accomplished a great deal both in terms of raising awareness of disproportionate exposures of people of colour and low-income people to environmental hazards, and by pressing policymakers in both the public sector and the private sector to take remedial action.

LP: Three states – Illinois, Ohio and Pennsylvania – account for 40 per cent of Congressional districts that appear in your top-ten rankings for inequality in industrial air pollution. What factors are impacting residents in those areas?

JB: Those states, broadly corresponding to the old industrial heartland of the country, are places where you have both relatively high levels of industrial air pollution and relatively high disparities. And so that makes them areas where environmental justice advocacy and enforcement activities should be high on the agenda of environmentalists, community activists and public officials.

LP: Do you think that your study will help activate politicians in those districts to address disparities?

JB: I would hope so. In terms of the policy relevance of our work, the methods we developed help to provide information about where pollution abatement efforts ought to be concentrated. What are the most important places where we should try to reduce community exposure to industrial air pollution? And insofar as new pollution sources are going to be constructed, where should they be built so as not to exacerbate the disparities that already plague so many communities?

LP: What are some of the most concerning economic effects of industrial air pollution on communities?

JB: Air pollution has adverse effects on people's health, and that means that they have to spend more on healthcare and that they miss more days of work, either because they themselves are too ill to go to work or because their kids are sick and they have to stay home and take care of them. It also has adverse effects on property values, which vary with the levels of air pollution in communities.

On top of these effects, pollution also impacts equality of opportunity, particularly for children. Communities that are heavily burdened with air pollution tend to have higher incidence and greater severity of childhood asthma, so the kids miss more days of school. And partly because they're missing school and perhaps partly because of the neurological impacts of air pollution on their young and developing cognitive functions, air pollution has an adverse effect on school performance.

If you believe, as I think most Americans believe, that every kid deserves an equal chance, that equality of opportunity for children is dear to our society for reasons of both equity and efficiency, then the impacts of disproportionate pollution burdens on the children in some communities – the fact that the playing field is tilted against them through no fault of their own – is a deeply troubling feature of our environmental landscape.

LP: You've noted that exposure contributes to student achievement gaps. Does this information challenge the assumption that the problems of education lie mostly with schools and teachers?

JB: Of course it does. What it suggests is that the playing field is not level and that not all teachers are teaching in the same environment. So even if teachers are equally qualified, and equally hard-working, educational outcomes will differ. A team of researchers led by Manuel Pastor of the University of Southern California looked at variations in school performance in the Los Angeles Unified School District. They controlled for the usual factors, such as parental income and education, class size and teacher salaries, and found that when they plugged in data on variations on air quality, it had a significant adverse effect on school performance.[2] What that implies is that even if one attended to every other educational problem, we'd still see disparities in educational outcomes as long as we have serious disparities in pollution exposure.

LP: How might we confront the environmental disparities you have highlighted?

JB: Well, I think there are a variety of strategies for doing so. A first step is to measure and map the extent of disparities, so that we have a handle on what the problem really is. Once we've got that information, there are a variety of things that individuals and communities can do to try to improve the situation.

One is to press public officials to take steps to redress excessive pollution burdens. Executive Order 12898 issued by President Clinton in 1994, which remains in force, directs all federal agencies to take steps to identify and rectify disproportionate health and environmental impacts resulting from their activities, policies and programmes on minorities and low-income populations. That mandate is already on the books at the federal level. Some states have EJ policies, too, and states that don't have them, ought to have them. Communities can press officials to act on those mandates, both to prevent additional pollution and to reduce existing burdens.

Above and beyond that, communities can directly engage with and, when necessary, confront, private-sector actors that are creating the pollution. Most firms are not insensitive to public opinion. In fact, firms may voluntarily take steps to clean up their act, if and when they realize that their communities are aware of what's going on.

This is why the public's right to know about environmental hazards is so important. An informed public can press both public officials and private firms to curtail pollution and to reduce environmental disparities.

LP : On the research front, what's left to be done?

JB : There are a host of interesting things that can and should be done. One important topic is the interface between inequalities in pollution exposure and the effort to transition to a cleaner and greener energy economy. As climate policy begins to get traction again, one very interesting question will be how can we try to maximize the air quality and public health co-benefits of reducing carbon emissions from burning fossil fuels.

When we reduce our use of fossil fuels through energy efficiency or conversion to renewable and cleaner energy sources, we not only cut emissions of carbon dioxide, the most important contributor to global climate change, but also reduce our emissions of many other air pollutants, such as particulate matter, sulfur dioxide, nitrogen oxides and a variety of air toxins. These reductions in hazardous air pollutants are sometimes called 'co-benefits' of climate policy.

These co-benefits turn out to be really substantial. A recent International Monetary Fund study of the top 20 carbon-emitting countries found that the public health co-benefits alone are enough to justify aggressive policies to phase out fossil fuels.[3] We need to design policies that will maximize the co-benefit bang for the clean energy buck, so to speak, and ensure that the reductions in co-pollutants are targeted to the communities that currently bear the highest pollution burdens.

Chapter 16

CLEANING THE AIR AND COOLING THE PLANET*

Reduced use of fossil fuels brings cleaner air as well as a cooler planet.

There is good news and bad news about the clean energy transition. The good news is that half of the new electric-generating capacity installed worldwide in 2008–2010 was renewable.[1] The bad news is that half wasn't.

To avoid rapid global warming and its attendant human and economic risks, we need to accelerate the transition. We need to do more than slow the growth in use of fossil fuels: we need to cut their use substantially. This will require significantly ramped-up investments worldwide in energy efficiency and clean energy.

One way to encourage this investment is to base public policies on the full range of benefits from reduced burning of fossil fuels – not only global benefits from reduced greenhouse gas emissions but also local benefits from reduced emissions of particulates, nitrogen oxides, sulfur dioxide, carbon monoxide, mercury, benzene and other toxic pollutants.

In the European Union, research has shown that the clean air benefits alone are sufficient to justify investments in energy efficiency and renewables. 'The welfare effects of climate policy seem to be positive,' a 2006 report for the Netherlands Environmental Agency concluded, '*even when the long-term benefits of avoided climate impacts are not taken into account*' (emphasis added).[2]

The clean air co-benefits of climate policy may be even greater elsewhere, in countries with less stringent air pollution controls than Europe. World Bank data indicate that in the United States the human health damages from particulate emissions are six times higher per ton of carbon dioxide than the average for Germany, France and the United Kingdom. In China, the ratio is more than ten times higher.[3]

---

* Co-authored with Manuel Pastor.

It would be ironic if energy policies designed to internalize the external costs of greenhouse gas emissions were to ignore the external costs of co-pollutants. But there is an important difference between the two. The benefits of reduced greenhouse gas emissions are global, whereas air quality benefits of reduced co-pollutant emissions are local.

The difference matters for three reasons:

Efficiency: From a climate change standpoint, it doesn't matter where emission reductions occur. From an air quality standpoint, it can matter a lot. Co-pollutant damages vary depending on the type of fossil fuel, pollution control technologies and the population density of the surrounding area. Efficient policy design would aim for greater emission reductions where the public health benefits are greater.

Equity: Low-income and minority communities often bear disproportionate pollution burdens. In the United States, for example, African Americans, Latinos and other minorities account for 50 per cent of the human health impacts from air toxics emissions from petroleum refineries, considerably more than their 31 per cent share in the national population. Air quality benefits are in the sweet spot where equity and efficiency intersect.

Political salience: Last but not least, the air quality benefits of reduced use of fossil fuels are immediate as well as local. For both reasons, they may be critical in building public support for clean energy policies. Neglecting these benefits in policy design would not only be tantamount to leaving healthcare dollars lying on the ground – or floating in the air – it also would mean foregoing crucial allies in the battle to curb the use of fossil fuels.

In our study 'Cooling the Planet, Clearing the Air', we outline a variety of ways to bring air quality benefits to bear on climate policy.[4] Specific locations can be designated as priority zones under a carbon pricing system, whether a tax or cap-and-permit system. Similarly, specific industrial facilities and sectors can be assigned priority for emission reductions. Community benefit funds can be established to channel some of the rent generated by carbon pricing into environmental and public health investments in overburdened communities.

In the twentieth century, environmentalists urged us to 'think globally, act locally'. As we embark on the clean energy transition of the twenty-first century, we need to think locally when acting globally, too.

Part III
CLIMATE POLICY

Chapter 17

SMART CLIMATE POLICY

Smart climate policy walks on three legs: public investment, carbon pricing and regulatory standards.

In a memorable moment in a memorable presidential campaign, candidate Barack Obama explained why he rejected John McCain's call to postpone their September debate in Oxford, Mississippi, during the negotiations on the first financial bailout package. 'It's going to be part of the President's job,' Obama declared, 'to be able to deal with more than one thing at once.'

Something similar can be said about climate policy. A variety of proposals – for public investment, carbon pricing, regulatory standards – are cooking in Washington's political stew. Sometimes the proponents of specific policies are tempted to oversell their merits, while dismissing other policies as unnecessary or even counterproductive. But if political leaders and policy wonks are going to get smart on climate change, part of their job is to deal with more than one policy instrument at once.

Climate change cannot be reduced to single-issue politics. The challenge of weaning the United States from its dependence on fossil fuels that spew carbon into the Earth's atmosphere is inseparable from the challenges of reviving its economy, generating decent jobs and restoring its leadership in the international community.

Nor can climate change be treated effectively as a single-policy issue. Public investment is crucial, but it will not solve the problem alone. Ditto carbon pricing. Ditto regulatory standards. Each must be part of the solution, and each will enhance the effectiveness of the others. Choosing more than one item from the toolkit is the essence of smart climate policy.

Public Investment

In 2009, with the economy in its deepest crisis since the Great Depression – at a time when banks weren't lending, firms weren't investing, consumers weren't spending and jobs were disappearing – a big programme of public investment occupied the centre of the political stage.

Public spending, unlike tax cuts, directly boosts demand for goods and services. And unlike private consumption, a sizeable fraction of which goes into buying imports, public spending can be targeted to spur demand for goods and services produced at home.

As critics are quick to point out, public spending can be wasteful in the sense of creating nothing of lasting value. The government can inject a short-run stimulus into the economy simply by paying people to dig holes in the ground and fill them up. If instead we pay people to build things of lasting value – that is, if we *invest* well and wisely – we can benefit twice, not only rebooting the economy in the short term but also strengthening the economy for the years ahead.

At this juncture in history, some of the most strategic public investments we can make are in energy efficiency and renewable energy. These investments are necessary, first and foremost, to insure our grandchildren against the threat of catastrophic climate change.

These investments will also reduce our reliance on imported oil and the regimes that supply it. At the same time, they will curtail the many other damages inflicted by the extraction and burning of fossil fuels, from 'mountaintop removal' in Appalachia to toxic air pollution in communities located near refineries and highways.

Dollar-for-dollar, investment in energy efficiency and renewable energy scores much higher in job creation than investment in fossil fuels. Every million dollars spent on retrofitting buildings generate 7 jobs directly, plus 11 more jobs indirectly through the purchases of supplies and consumption by the workers – 18 jobs in total. In mass transit and freight rail, the total is even higher: nearly 22 jobs per $1 million spending. The corresponding total in the coal industry is 9 jobs. In oil and gas, it's even less: fewer than 6 jobs per $1 million.[1]

Public investments, and the private investments 'crowded in' by public investments, can not only spur net job growth but also target areas of the country where job creation is most needed – including areas that will experience losses of jobs in the fossil fuel industries as we move to the post-carbon economy of the future.

The 'green recovery program' proposed by my colleagues at the Political Economy Research Institute calls for public investment in retrofitting buildings, mass transit and freight rail, a 'smart' electrical grid, wind and solar power, next-generation biofuels and loan guarantees to encourage more private investment in energy efficiency and renewables. The stimulus bill signed into law by President Obama in 2009 contained similar provisions.

By definition, a stimulus programme increases demand for goods and services rather than simply reshuffling demand from one sector of the economy to another. Public investment in a stimulus package is not financed by taxes, or sales of carbon permits, or cuts in other public expenditures: it is financed by deficit spending, including both borrowing and Federal Reserve purchases of Treasury bills (or 'printing money' in the language of the pre-electronic era).

When the economy recovers and stimulus spending draws down, we need to find other ways to pay for ongoing public investments in the clean energy transition. One possibility is to reallocate the federal subsidies currently lavished upon the oil, coal and natural gas industries. Whether Washington will have the political stomach to end these handouts is an open question. But it makes no sense to subsidize with one hand the same activities that we are trying to phase out with the other.

Carbon Pricing

Putting a price on carbon is a second key element of smart climate policy. An underlying reason for our current situation is that we have treated Earth's limited capacity to absorb and recycle carbon emissions as if it was infinite. When useful things are in infinite supply, they're free. When useful things are scarce, they have a price. To send the right market signals to consumers and producers, we need to correct this mistake by putting a price on carbon emissions.

There are two ways to do so. The first is to levy a carbon tax (or fee), set as a fixed dollar amount per ton of carbon emissions. The quantity of emissions will vary depending on demand and the business cycle, but it will certainly be lower than in the absence of tax.

The second way to price carbon is to put a cap on the total quantity of emissions, an objective most easily achieved by limiting the amount of carbon entering the economy in coal, oil and natural gas. A fixed number of permits, their total quantity being set by the cap, are made available to the firms that extract fossil fuels at home or import them from abroad. The permits could be given away free or they could be auctioned at the price set by market demand.

No matter whether carbon permits are given away, auctioned or distributed by some mix of the two methods, an inevitable effect of a cap (and, likewise, of a carbon tax) is a rise in the prices of gasoline, heating oil, natural gas, coal-fired electricity and everything that uses fossil fuels in its production or distribution. In other words, the permit price (or tax) is passed through to the end users. This is Economics 101: lower supply results in a higher price. These higher prices give firms and households a stronger incentive to invest in energy efficiency and alternative fuels.

The price hikes that come with carbon pricing are a cost to individual consumers but not a cost to the economy as a whole. The reason is that every dollar paid in higher prices winds up in someone else's hands, with no extra resources being used to produce the goods and services being bought. In economic terminology, the result of carbon pricing is a 'transfer', not a 'resource cost'. This poses the trillion-dollar question: Who gets the money?

The answer depends on the design of the policy. The money could go to energy corporations as windfall profits. It could go to the government as revenue from permit sales or taxes. It could be refunded to the public as equal payments to every person in the country. Or it could be disbursed via some combination of the three.

The windfall profit scenario is what happens if carbon permits are simply given away for free to corporations, who then are free to buy and sell them to each other in a permit market – a policy known as 'cap and trade'. Prices at the pump will rise regardless of whether permits are auctioned or given away – just as rents in housing markets are the same regardless of whether the owner paid for the house or inherited it. Under the giveaway option, energy corporations 'inherit' the new property rights created by carbon permits (the property in question being the carbon absorptive capacity of the planet). In effect, this option legitimizes the prior capture of this scarce resource by polluters.

The government revenue scenario is attractive to those seeking ways to fund new or existing government programmes, including public investment in the clean energy transition. However, what the government will actually do with the money is always an open question, the answer to which will change with shifts in the political climate. Under this option, the new property rights belong to the government, which collects the carbon rent.

The public refund scenario, often called 'carbon dividends', is attracting increasing attention in Congress and the media. Instead of being treated as government revenue, the money from permit auctions (or carbon taxes) is deposited into a stand-alone trust fund, akin to the Social Security trust fund, from which dividends are paid to the public (for example, in quarterly installments). The simplest way to do this is to issue 'Carbon Trust Cards' that can be used like ATM cards to check individual balances and withdraw cash – a system that is already available for Social Security payments. Under this option, rights to the Earth's capacity to absorb carbon belong equally to all.

In the latter two scenarios, there is no need for permit trading. Carbon permits would be purchased at auction by the firms that want them. Like other, more familiar sorts of permits – building permits, parking permits, driver's licenses – they would not have to be tradable. The need for tradable permits arises only if permits are given away free to corporations (based on their historic emissions or some other formula), leading to situations where some firms wind up with more permits than they need, others with fewer, and trading is needed to get an efficient allocation. If the permits instead are auctioned, we get the same efficient outcome without the added cost of traders' profit margins and without the risks of speculation and market manipulation.

Apart from the philosophical appeal of the premise that the gifts of Nature belong equally to all persons, a compelling political case can be made for the dividend option. Carbon pricing will be politically sustainable only if the higher fuel prices that result do not spark a furious backlash from a public already hard-pressed to make ends meet. While attending U.N. climate talks in Poznan, Poland, in December 2008, Wisconsin congressman James Sensenbrenner, the ranking Republican on the House Select Committee on Energy Independence and Global Warming, spelled out the political implications: '[I]f people on the other side of the aisle want to push a doubling to tripling of electricity bills and $10 a gallon gas, I can guarantee you that the Republicans may very well be in the majority after the 2010 election.'[2]

While $10/gallon gasoline is not imminent under any likely policy scenario in the United States, there can be little doubt that any serious effort to curtail fossil fuel consumption will mean higher prices for gasoline, heating oil and coal-fired electricity. How much higher will depend on the tightness of the emissions cap, the state of the economy (in a recession the price increase will be less than during an economic boom) and the extent to which complementary investments and regulatory policies reduce demand for fossil fuels. But unless and until the transition to the post-carbon economy is well underway, carbon-pricing policies will surely translate into higher fuel prices.

There is one and only one way to avoid a public backlash against higher prices for gasoline, heating oil and electricity: refund the money to the people. Equal per-person refunds will fully offset the impact of higher fuel prices on the budget of the average household. At the same time, higher fuel prices will give everyone an incentive to economize on fuel consumption. Households with lower-than-average carbon footprints – including most low-income households, because they consume less of just about everything – come out ahead in monetary terms, not even counting the benefits of saving the planet. The only way I can imagine to make Americans happy about higher prices at the pump is to give them certain knowledge that those prices mean more money in their pockets.

Smart Regulatory Standards

The third leg of smart climate policy, alongside public investment and carbon pricing, is regulatory standards. Before the 2008 financial meltdown, 'regulation' was often treated as a dirty word in American politics. It was rehabilitated when it became evident that without rules (a.k.a. regulations), the logic of self-interest can run amok, turning Adam Smith's celebrated 'invisible hand' into a colossal pickpocket.

To say that rules are necessary is not, of course, to say that all rules are good. As critics are quick to point out, some regulations are of questionable benefit, and some are pretty dumb. This is not an argument against regulation across the board. It is an argument for smart regulatory standards.

Smart regulatory standards are an important part of smart climate policy for three reasons. First, 'getting prices right' through permits or carbon taxes will not automatically ensure that the private sector makes all of the desirable and feasible investments in energy efficiency and renewables. The market works only when investors are smart enough to read the market-signal tea leaves. One thing we have learned from the history of the American automobile industry in recent decades is that some folks – including some very powerful market players – are remarkably obtuse. When myopia, inertia, ignorance or just plain stupidity dim the power of price signals, we need to use the power of rules.

Energy experts have long pointed out the paradoxical fact that there is much scope for energy-saving investments that would quickly pay for themselves, including building insulation and more efficient lighting, heating, air conditioning and appliances. A December 2007 study by the consulting firm McKinsey & Co. found that substantial reductions in the US carbon emissions could be achieved at *negative cost* simply by taking advantage of existing opportunities at existing prices.[3] If the magic of the market were all that was needed, these profitable options wouldn't exist – they would already have been fully exploited.

Fuel efficiency standards for automobiles, energy efficiency standards for appliances and 'green' building costs are examples of regulatory standards that can kick in when market players fail to read the price signals.

The second reason we need smart regulatory standards is to take account of social benefits and costs that are not calculated in the price signals of the marketplace. Even with carbon pricing, for example, wind and solar-generated electricity may not be competitive in many locations until their costs are brought down by further research and development and greater economies of scale in production. In the meantime, we can learn from countries such as Germany and Spain that have enacted rules that require utilities to buy power from small-scale generators at remunerative 'feed-in tariff' prices.

Similarly, one way to boost private investment for renewables and energy efficiency is to channel bank lending towards green projects through asset-based reserve requirements, stipulating that a certain percentage of every bank's loan portfolio should be channelled to such purposes. If 5 per cent of private lending in the United States were channelled into green investments, this would amount to roughly $100 billion per year.[4]

The third reason to include regulatory standards in the climate policy mix is that we need to curb not only carbon emissions but also other environmental damages caused by the fossil fuel industry. From the standpoint of climate change, all carbon dioxide emissions are equal; it doesn't matter where they are reduced. From the standpoint of human health, however, it can matter a great deal. Some places – often communities with high percentages of minorities and low-income families – are severely affected by dirty air, contaminated water and devastated landscapes that result from activities such as oil refining and coal mining. It makes economic as well as moral sense to target the carbon reductions to the locations where the 'co-benefits' of these reductions are greatest. Smart regulatory standards on airborne particulate matter, toxic air and water pollution, and environmentally destructive mining practices are a vital ingredient of smart climate policy.

No country can solve the problem of global warming on its own. Global problems require global solutions. Along with other industrialized countries, the United States has the responsibility and capacity to help developing countries shift to a low-carbon growth path. To become a credible leader in the global struggle against climate change, the United States must begin by implementing a smart climate policy at home.

Chapter 18

INVESTMENT IN DISADVANTAGED COMMUNITIES

Community benefit funds that channel carbon revenues into environmental investments in disadvantaged communities can promote both equity and efficiency. Based on a memorandum written for the Economics and Allocation Advisory Committee of the California Air Resources Board and California Environmental Protection Agency.

The California Global Warming Solutions Act of 2006 (Assembly Bill 32) mandates that the California Air Resources Board (CARB) should seek to channel investment to the state's most disadvantaged communities:

The state board shall ensure that the greenhouse gas emission reduction rules, regulations, programs, mechanisms, and incentives under its jurisdiction, where applicable and to the extent feasible, direct public and private investment toward the most disadvantaged communities in California and provide an opportunity for small businesses, schools, affordable housing associations, and other community institutions to participate in and benefit from statewide efforts to reduce greenhouse gas emissions.

In addition, the Act mandates that CARB should consider localized impacts of co-pollutants that are emitted along with carbon dioxide when fossil fuels are burned:

Prior to the inclusion of any market-based compliance mechanism in the regulations, to the extent feasible and in furtherance of achieving the statewide greenhouse gas emissions limit, the state board shall do all of the following: (1) Consider the potential for direct, indirect, and cumulative emission impacts from these mechanisms, including localized impacts in communities that are already adversely impacted by air pollution. (2) Design any market-based compliance mechanism to prevent any increase in the emissions of toxic air contaminants or criteria air pollutants.

Disadvantaged communities often are disproportionately impacted by air pollutants, including co-pollutants generated by the use of fossil fuels. One way to fulfill these mandates is to allocate a share of allowance value (that is, revenue from auctions of carbon emission permits) to these communities for the purpose of environmental improvements.

This use of allowance value primarily involves investment, but it also can be considered a form of compensation in that a community's eligibility to receive benefits rests on its disadvantaged status, including disproportionate pollution exposure. Eligibility for compensation does not require that AB 32 causes an increase in co-pollutants in the localities – an outcome specifically prohibited in the section of the Act quoted above – but rather that disproportionate impacts *relative to other localities* persist after AB 32 implementation. The aim is to mitigate gaps in environmental and economic well-being in disadvantaged localities relative to statewide norms.

Co-pollutants and the co-benefits from their reduction are relevant to the efficiency, environmental and fairness objectives of AB 32.

Efficiency

The efficiency objective implies that policy should seek to maximize net social benefits from reducing greenhouse gas emissions. These benefits include co-pollutant reductions. To ignore them would be tantamount to leaving healthcare dollars lying on the ground.

From a climate-change standpoint, the marginal benefit of carbon reductions is constant across emission sources. But in the presence of co-pollutants – such as particulate matter, nitrogen oxides and air toxics released by the burning of fossil fuels – the marginal benefit can and does vary across emission sources.

Variations in marginal abatement costs across pollution sources provide the static-efficiency rationale for using carbon prices to reduce emissions, as opposed to relying exclusively on regulatory standards. The aim is to achieve pollution reductions at least total cost.

But variations in marginal abatement benefits complicate the picture. These provide a rationale for greater pollution reductions (and higher marginal abatement costs) for some emission sources than for others.

A 2009 study by the National Academy of Sciences estimates that the burning of fossil fuels in the United States is responsible for roughly 20,000 premature deaths each year, translating into more than $100 billion/year in health damages.[1] This estimate is based on the effects of criteria air pollutants and does not include damages from climate change or harm to ecosystems.

In addition to improvements in the quantity and quality of life, benefits from co-pollutant reductions include healthcare cost savings, reductions in days lost from work due to illness and the need to care for ill children and other dependents, and gains in property values.

In economic terms, the co-benefits from co-pollutant reduction add to the benefits from reduced carbon dioxide emissions. This justifies greater reductions (tighter caps, higher permit prices and higher marginal abatement costs) than would be warranted in the absence of co-benefits.

If co-pollutant intensity – the ratio of co-pollutant damages to carbon dioxide emissions – were a fixed coefficient, there would be no efficiency case for modifying policy design (beyond adjusting the overall cap) to take co-pollutants into account. But there are strong *a priori* reasons to expect that co-pollutant intensity varies across regions, sectors and polluters, and empirical evidence supports this view.

The ratio of co-pollutant emissions to carbon dioxide emissions varies depending on the fuel source (higher for coal, lower for natural gas, in-between for oil) and pollution control technologies. In addition, damages per unit of co-pollutant emissions vary depending, among other things, on stack heights, population densities and total exposure.

From the standpoint of efficiency, the existence of co-pollutants implies not only that the overall cap on carbon emissions should be tighter than what would be warranted by the environmental impacts of carbon dioxide alone but also that policy design should respond to variations in co-pollution intensity.

Environment

The environmental objective refers to the full range of pollution-reduction benefits that AB 32 implementation can bring about. The Act explicitly sets this forth:

> *It is the intent of the Legislature that the State Air Resources Board design emissions reduction measures to meet the statewide emissions limits for greenhouse gases established pursuant to this division in a manner that minimizes costs and maximizes benefits for California's economy, improves and modernizes California's energy infrastructure and maintains electric system reliability, maximizes additional environmental and economic co-benefits for California, and complements the state's efforts to improve air quality.*

Among possible uses of revenue generated under AB 32, CARB's December 2008 Scoping Plan includes the following:

> *Achieving environmental co-benefits: Criteria and toxic air pollutants create health risks, and some communities bear a disproportionate burden from air pollution. Revenues could be used*

to enhance greenhouse gas emission reductions that also provide reductions in air and other pollutants that affect public health.[2]

Fairness

The fairness objective implies that policy should seek to reduce disproportionate pollution in historically overburdened communities. For this reason, the issue of co-pollutants has been emphasized by the California's Environmental Justice Advisory Committee.

If co-pollutants were uniformly (or randomly) distributed across the landscape, there would be no fairness reason to design policy to take them into account. But again, both *a priori* reasoning and empirical evidence tell us that they are not uniformly distributed, and that some communities – often lower-income and minority communities – are overburdened by co-pollutants.

CARB's development of a methodology using available information 'to assess the potential cumulative air pollution impacts of proposed regulations to implement the Scoping Plan' and 'to identify communities already adversely impacted by air pollution' can be used to design policies consistent with the fairness objective.[3]

Policy options

Four types of policies can be implemented in order to advance the efficiency, environmental, and fairness objectives of AB 32 in relation to co-pollutants: (1) investment by allocating allowance value to a Community Benefit Fund (CBF); (2) a co-pollutant surcharge; (3) zonal trading systems; and (4) priority facility designations.

Community Benefit Fund

One way to tackle co-pollutant issues is to allocate part of the revenue from permit auctions to overburdened communities, dedicating the money for environmental improvements. In its Final Report, the Economic and Technology Advancement Advisory Committee recommended this as one use of auction revenues (which it proposed be routed through a California Carbon Trust):

By setting aside a fixed portion of its funds to be distributed to projects based on cumulative impacts, geographic location, demographics, and/or associated co- benefits, this Trust could also help to reach important environmental justice goals. Distributing funds based on geography or demography would ensure that disadvantaged communities receive a pre-determined amount of funding from projects that not only reduce carbon emissions, but also foster community development and protect low income consumers from rising energy prices.[4]

Issues in developing and implementing such a policy include: how much revenue (or what percentage of allowance value) to allocate to CBFs; which communities are eligible to receive funds; what sorts of environmental projects are eligible; and what mechanisms should be established to allocate funds across and within communities.

Co-pollutant Surcharge

A second way to incorporate co-pollutants into the AB 32 implementation policy is to levy a surcharge on carbon permits in overburdened jurisdictions, and to dedicate the surcharge revenue to CBFs in the same jurisdictions where it is collected.

Attractive features of this option include the following:

- The use of surcharge revenue for this purpose would reduce the need to allocate revenues from carbon permit auctions to CBFs.
- There would be a tight nexus between the fee (surcharge) and its use.
- The surcharge would promote greater emission reductions in places where abatement benefits are greater due to high co-pollutant burdens.
- It affirms the principle that the 'sink' functions of the air (as a medium for disposal of wastes) belong to the people who breathe it.

To implement such a system, CARB would again identify overburdened locations where the co-pollutant surcharge would be levied, at the time of carbon permit surrender in the case of stationary sources or at the time of fuel delivery in the case of residential and mobile sources. By increasing the price of fossil fuels above what it would be in the absence of the surcharge, this would provide an incentive for greater emissions reductions in these locations.

Zonal Trading Systems

A third way to include co-benefits from co-pollutant reductions in cap-and-trade policy design is to establish zones to guarantee some minimum level of emissions reductions in high-priority locations where co-benefits are greatest.

In zonal trading systems, the availability of permits is defined on a zone-by-zone basis, that is, permits are allocated across zones within the overall cap. Zone-based 'sub-caps' can be established regardless of whether permits are distributed via auction, free allowances or some combination of the two.

The zones create semipermeable boundaries for permit trading: polluters in lower-priority zones can buy permits from polluters in higher-priority zones, but permit trades against this gradient are not allowed.[5]

A zonal system need not be restricted to point-source emissions: it could be applied to mobile sources, too, which account for a large share of emissions of some co-pollutants. Just as AB 32 effectively makes the state of California into a 'zone' where carbon emissions from both point sources and mobile sources are capped differentially from other states, so a zonal system can differentiate across regions or localities within the state.

One precedent for a zonal trading system is California's Regional Clean Air Incentives Market (RECLAIM), launched in 1994 to reduce point-source emissions of nitrogen oxides and sulfur oxides in the Los Angeles basin. The South Coast Air Quality Management District established two zones under RECLAIM: zone 1, the coastal zone, where pollution is more severe and the benefits from pollution reduction are considered to be greater; and zone 2, the inland zone, where pollution is less severe. Facilities in zone 1 can buy permits only from other facilities in the same zone; facilities in zone 2 can buy permits from either zone. One impact of the RECLAIM zonal trading system is that average permit prices have been roughly eight times higher in zone 1 than in zone 2.[6]

A zonal trading system – whether comprising two zones as in RECLAIM, or several – cannot, of course, perfectly match marginal abatement costs to all variations across pollution sources in marginal abatement benefits. Within any zone, some variations will persist. But the question is not whether a zonal trading system yields textbook efficiency; it is whether it yields a better outcome in terms of environmental, efficiency and equity criteria than a system without zones. When externalities are spatially differentiated – that is, when emission location matters – zonal trading systems can be a 'second-best' solution that yields a better outcome than the no-zone alternative.[7]

Priority Facility or Sector Designations

A fourth option is to identify specific facilities or sectors that emit high levels of co-pollutants and/or make the most significant contributions to co-pollutant burdens in disadvantaged communities, and to designate these as priority facilities or sectors for carbon emission reductions.[8] Similar to zonal trading systems, within the overall cap the priority designation would establish sub-caps on the number of permits available to individual facilities or facilities in a specific sector. Again, the policy would create a semipermeable boundary: other polluters can buy permits from designated priority facilities, but not vice versa. Similarly, the purchase of offsets by priority facilities would be constrained or proscribed.

This option takes advantage of the phenomenon known as 'disproportionality' in environmental impacts: a few facilities with much higher-than-average impacts often account for a large fraction of the total impact.[9] By targeting a relatively small number of facilities that account for a relatively large share of co-pollutant damages in disadvantaged communities, this policy could achieve a large payoff while economizing on administrative burdens.

Concluding Remarks

Policies to reduce carbon dioxide emissions from burning fossil fuels generate co-benefits above and beyond their climate-change benefits, by reducing emissions of co-pollutants that harm human health. Damages from co-pollutants per unit carbon dioxide emissions vary across locations and pollution sources. Historically overburdened communities tend to be economically and socially disadvantaged in other respects as well. Hence the objectives of AB 32 can be furthered by policies that take co-pollutants and co-benefits into account.

Here I have sketched four policy options:

- allocating some fraction of allowance value to community benefit funds (CBFs);
- introducing a co-pollutant surcharge, with the proceeds dedicated to CBFs;
- establishing a zonal trading system that restricts the ability of polluters in high-priority localities from 'buying out' of emission-reduction obligations by purchasing offsets or permits from other localities; and
- designating priority facilities or sectors for co-pollutant reductions, with restrictions on their ability to purchase offsets or permits from other polluters.

These options are not mutually exclusive. Rather they can be seen as complementary ways to advance a common set of goals: efficiency, environmental protection and fairness.

Chapter 19

DIVIDENDS FOR ALL

California can use carbon revenues to build durable public support for its pioneering effort to wean the state's economy from fossil fuels. Based on a memorandum written for the Economics and Allocation Advisory Committee (EAAC) of the California Air Resources Board and California Environmental Protection Agency.

The return of carbon permit auction revenues as equal per capita dividends to the public is sometimes termed 'cap-and-dividend'. This policy option was singled out in Governor Schwarzenegger's 22 May 2009 letter to the EAAC:

There is one idea in particular I would like you to explore among other options: the concept of returning the value of allowances back to the people, including through an auction of allowances and distribution of auction proceeds in the form of a rebate or dividend.

There are three fundamental rationales for cap-and-dividend.

The principle of common ownership of nature's wealth: A consequence of any policy to limit use of a resource – to manage scarcity – is the creation of property rights. Cap-and-dividend starts from the premise that rights to the property created by the introduction of carbon permits belong in common and equal measure to all.[1] Cap-and-dividend is a 'feebate' arrangement in which individuals pay fees based on their use of a scarce resource that they own in common, and the fees are then rebated in equal measure to all co-owners. In this case, the scarce resource is the California's share of the carbon storage capacity of the atmosphere; the fee is set by the carbon footprint of each household; and the co-owners are the people of the state.

Protection of household real incomes: A second rationale is to protect the real incomes of households from the impact of higher fossil fuel prices resulting from the cap. If the amount paid by households in higher prices is returned as dividends, the household sector as a whole is made whole by the policy. The net impact on any individual household varies depending on its carbon footprint. Those with larger-than-average carbon footprints pay more than they receive in dividends; those with smaller-than-average carbon footprints receive more than they pay. Since carbon footprints are correlated with income, lower-income and middle-income families generally receive greater net benefits from the policy than upper-income households. Across the entire income spectrum, however, every household has an incentive to reduce its carbon footprint in response to market price signals: those who reduce them most obtain the greatest net monetary gain.

Securing durable public support for the carbon policy: A cap on carbon emissions will increase the prices of gasoline, electricity and other commodities in proportion to their carbon content. A cap that does not have this effect is not a binding cap. For political sustainability, it is important to anticipate public reactions to higher fuel prices and to craft a policy design that voters will accept or, better yet, positively welcome. Cap-and-dividend's democratic premise – that California's share of the atmosphere's carbon-absorptive capacity belongs to its people – and its visible contribution to family incomes may improve the carbon policy's prospects for survival over the long haul.

Precedents

Three precedents for a cap-and-dividend policy are the Alaska Permanent Fund, which distributes dividends from oil revenues equally to all residents of that state; the 'Climate Change Consumer Refund Account' provision of the American Clean Energy and Security Act (ACES, also known as the Waxman-Markey bill), passed by the US House of Representatives in June 2009; and the 'Carbon Refund Trust Fund' of the Carbon Limits and Energy for America's Renewal (CLEAR) Act, introduced by US Senators Maria Cantwell and Susan Collins in December 2009.

The *Alaska Permanent Fund,* established in 1976 under the leadership of Governor Jay Hammond, recycles the state's oil-extraction royalties to the public as equal per-person dividends. In 2008 the dividend per capita amounted to $2,069 (in addition to a one-time 'resource rebate' of $1,200). Apart from operationalizing the core principle of common and equal ownership of natural wealth, the Fund demonstrates that it is administratively feasible for state governments to define eligibility and disburse dividends to residents. A major difference, of course, is that the Alaska Permanent Fund gives residents an incentive to support higher oil extraction, whereas cap-and-dividend results in the opposite incentive: a tighter cap yields increased dividends (assuming inelastic demand for fossil fuels, that is, a 10 per cent increase in prices is associated with a less than 10 per cent reduction in demand, and hence higher total revenue).

The *Climate Change Consumer Refund Account* proposed in section 789(a) of the ACES bill provides that:

In each year after deposits are made to the Climate Change Consumer Refund Account, the Secretary of the Treasury shall provide tax refunds on a per capita basis to each household in the United States that shall collectively equal the amount deposited into the Climate Change Consumer Refund Account.

The share of the Climate Change Refund Account in the proposed allocation of allowance value in ACES rises over time. The refund begins in the 2020s and grows to about 50 per cent of allowance value in the 2030s and 2040s. While ACES is not a cap-and-dividend policy in its initial years, it substantially turns into one over time.

The *Carbon Refund Trust Fund* proposed in the CLEAR Act would return 75 per cent of allowance value to households as monthly per capita dividends. The remaining 25 per cent is devoted to investments in energy efficiency, clean energy, adaptation to climate change and transitional adjustment assistance.

Distributional Impacts of Carbon Pricing

The gross cost to a household from carbon pricing is a function of the amount of fossil carbon embodied in the production and distribution of the goods and services it consumes (the household's 'carbon footprint'). The breakdown across expenditure categories for the median California household is shown in Figure 19.1.

Because lower-income households generally consume less than higher-income households, they typically have smaller carbon footprints. In the highest decile, carbon emissions per capita are roughly six times greater than in the lowest decile.

As a *share* of their income, however, the poor consume more carbon than the rich – that is, more carbon per dollar. This is largely because fuels and electricity account for a larger share of their household budgets, whereas upper-income groups spend a higher share on other items. In the absence of offsetting transfers of allowance value, putting a price on carbon therefore is regressive: the higher prices arising from the introduction of carbon permits take a larger share of income from the poor than from households in upper-income brackets.

Table 19.1 shows the breakdown of carbon footprints by income decile and expenditure category. Direct fuel consumption looms larger in the expenditure basket of low-income households, accounting for 69 per cent of the total carbon footprint in the lowest decile. In the highest decile, by contrast, indirect consumption (via other goods and services) accounts for more than half of the total carbon footprint.

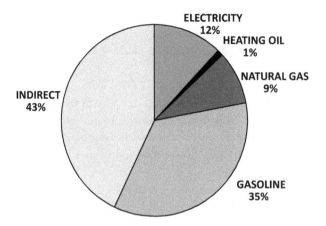

Figure 19.1 Carbon footprint by expenditure category: Median California household **Direct energy consumption accounts for more than half of the carbon emissions of the median California household, with gasoline alone accounting for more than one-third.** Indirect emissions come from expenditures on other goods and services that use fossil fuels in their production or distribution. *Source:* Calculated using the methodology of J. K. Boyce and M. Riddle, 'Cap and Dividend: A State-by-State Analysis'. Amherst, MA: Political Economy Research Institute, August 2009.

Distributional Impacts of Cap-and-Dividend

Because gross costs to households are based on their carbon footprints, while dividends are paid equally to all, the *net impact* of cap-and-dividend is distributionally progressive. Table 19.2 illustrates this point, showing how California households would be affected by a *national* cap-and-dividend policy with a permit price of $25/ton carbon dioxide, 100 per cent of permits auctioned and 80 per cent of auction revenue returned as dividends. In this scenario, lower-income deciles see substantial net benefits; middle-income deciles are 'kept whole' with dividends more than offsetting the impact of higher fuel prices; and the top two deciles see net costs. Overall, roughly eight in ten California households come out ahead in monetary terms – without counting the environmental benefits that are, of course, the policy's main objective.

A *California-only* cap-and-dividend policy will yield somewhat different numbers than a national policy, even with the same carbon price and same revenue-allocation parameters, among other reasons because the carbon footprint of the average California resident is below the national average, largely due to energy efficiency policies that have reduced per capita electricity consumption, so that Californians fare better than average in a nationwide policy.

Table 19.1 Carbon footprint by income decile and expenditure category in California (metric tons CO_2 per person per year)

Income decile	Income per capita ($/yr)	Carbon footprint per capita (metric tons CO_2 per person per year)					
		Electricity	Gasoline	Natural gas	Heating oil	Other goods and services	Total
1	3788	0.78	1.41	0.49	0.07	1.21	3.96
2	6545	0.97	2.15	0.66	0.09	1.84	5.71
3	9062	1.09	2.69	0.77	0.10	2.38	7.03
4	11752	1.20	3.16	0.86	0.11	2.92	8.26
5	14841	1.31	3.61	0.95	0.12	3.52	9.51
6	18603	1.42	4.07	1.03	0.12	4.23	10.87
7	23494	1.54	4.55	1.12	0.13	5.12	12.46
8	30469	1.68	5.08	1.22	0.14	6.35	14.47
9	42186	1.87	5.71	1.33	0.16	8.35	17.43
10	72895	2.22	6.63	1.51	0.18	13.36	23.90
Mean	24889	1.41	3.91	0.99	0.12	5.10	11.54
Median	16616	1.37	3.84	0.99	0.12	3.86	10.17

Source: Calculated using the methodology of J. K. Boyce and M. Riddle, 'Cap and Dividend: A State-by-State Analysis'. Amherst, MA: Political Economy Research Institute, August 2009.

Table 19.2 Impact of national cap-and-dividend policy on California households by income decile ($25/tCO$_2$; 100% auction; 80% of revenue distributed as dividends)

Per capita income decile	Per capita income	$ per capita		Net impact	% of income		Net impact
		Carbon charge	Dividend		Carbon charge	Dividend	
1	3788	108	386	278	2.90	10.20	7.30
2	6545	149	386	237	2.20	5.90	3.60
3	9062	179	386	207	1.90	4.30	2.30
4	11752	207	386	179	1.70	3.30	1.50
5	14841	236	386	150	1.50	2.60	1.00
6	18603	268	386	118	1.40	2.10	0.60
7	23494	305	386	81	1.20	1.60	0.30
8	30469	354	386	32	1.10	1.30	0.10
9	42186	426	386	−40	0.90	0.90	−0.10
10	72895	593	386	−207	0.80	0.50	−0.30

Source: J. K. Boyce and M. Riddle, 'Cap and Dividend: A State-by-State Analysis'. Amherst, MA: Political Economy Research Institute, August 2009, Tables 3, 4, 5 and A.1.

But the broad pattern would persist: lower-income households gain, the middle class is protected and upper-income groups bear a net cost.[2]

Outcomes for individual households could differ from these broad patterns. In any income bracket, those who respond more strongly to the market price signals produced by the cap will fare better than those who do not curb consumption of fossil fuels. Upper-income households with carbon footprints below the norm for their bracket could get positive net benefits; lower and middle-income households with disproportionately large carbon footprints could come out behind.

Criticisms

Criticisms of carbon dividends fall into three classes: (1) other priorities for revenue (or allowance value) allocation, (2) universal coverage versus targeted beneficiaries and (3) regional disparities.

Other priorities include all non-dividend allocations of allowance value whether via free permits or auction revenue uses. Some of these are transitional in nature: compensation and some investment uses are in this category. Some are more permanent: general government revenue is in this category. In the case of transitional priorities, the policy mix between dividend and non-dividend allocations could change over time with the share allocated to dividends gradually increasing, as in ACES.

Universal coverage of dividends is sometimes criticized on the grounds that they would be received by some people who 'don't need them'. The Center for Budget and Policy Priorities has proposed instead that dividends be targeted to low-income households.[3] A provision for refunds to low-income consumers in ACES (Section 782(d)) embodies this approach. Targeted payments may be viewed as an adequate response to the compensation rationale for dividends. But they do not respond to the common ownership rationale. Universal coverage also may have political appeal; witness the durable public support for Social Security. In addition, means-testing for eligibility would impose extra administrative costs.

Regional disparities result from cap-and-dividend when carbon footprints differ by location. At the national level, inter-state disparities in net impacts are modest, and much smaller than those of other federal policies including defence spending and farm programmes.[4] Within California, differences in the carbon intensity of the electricity supply would contribute to regional disparities, but these are modest since electricity accounts for only 12 per cent of the median household's carbon footprint. Moreover, any regional disparities come from carbon pricing itself – not from dividends – so they are equally pertinent to other policies for allocation of allowance value.

Logistics of Dividend Eligibility and Disbursement

Eligibility for dividends will need to be defined (as, for example, the state has done in establishing residency requirements for in-state tuition at public universities). In the case of the Alaska Permanent Fund, which has more than 25 years of experience in distributing per capita dividends, in order to be eligible a person must have been an Alaska resident for the entire preceding calendar year (or, in the case of infants, must have been born during that year and have an eligible Alaska resident sponsor). Applicants for dividends in Alaska supply a Social Security Number and other identification information.[5]

Dividends can be disbursed via electronic benefit transfer (EBT) cards, direct deposits into bank accounts, cheques in the mail, or tax refunds. The first two methods – together known as electronic funds transfer – are widely used by federal and state agencies to distribute recurring payments to individuals; today more than 80 per cent of federal benefit payments are disbursed electronically. For example, EBT cards are widely used for Social Security payments and are the primary delivery vehicle for food stamp payments.[6]

Cheques in the mail are a costlier way to deliver payments but may be preferred by some individuals. Tax refunds require that the recipient file a tax return, so this method would be likely to result in some gaps in coverage. In addition, tax refunds as a means of dividend disbursement are less visible to recipients than the other disbursement methods and hence may be less effective as a way to maintain durable public support in the face of rising fossil fuel prices. For this reason, how the dividends are delivered is not merely a technical issue: it could prove crucial for the long-term success of the policy.

Chapter 20

TRUTH SPILL

The BP oil spill in the Gulf of Mexico brought home the true cost of the fossil fuels.

'An upside-down faucet, just open and running out.' That's how an oil-spill expert at the Woods Hole Oceanographic Institute described the massive release of crude oil into the Gulf of Mexico that began on 20 April 2010 at the British Petroleum (BP) Deep Horizon oil rig off the coast of Louisiana.[1]

The disaster opened an information faucet, too: every day, more truth about the real costs of fossil fuels emptied into public view. Desperate efforts to control both spills quickly were underway.

After its 450-ton blowout preventer failed, BP tried burning the oil slick, creating the macabre spectacle of the ocean on fire.[2] The company then tried using chemical dispersants to reduce the amount of oil reaching the surface, a strategy that helped to create enormous underwater oil plumes as much as 10 miles long, 3 miles wide and 300 feet thick.[3] The dispersants themselves are toxic, but their impacts on marine ecosystems are poorly understood because the chemical recipe is a proprietary secret.[4]

In exploration plans filed with the US government's ethically challenged Minerals Management Service[5] in February 2009, BP claimed it was 'unlikely that an accidental surface or subsurface oil spill would occur from the proposed activities', and that if this happened, 'due to the distance to shore (48 miles) and the response capabilities that would be implemented, no significant adverse impacts are expected'.[6] Three months later, oil had washed onto 65 miles of Louisiana's shoreline, penetrating more than 10 miles into coastal marshes that account for 40 per cent of the wetlands in the continental United States.[7] Fishing had been banned in 19 per cent of Gulf waters under US jurisdiction – a devastating blow to local livelihoods.[8]

Containing the truth spill proved to be as difficult as plugging the gusher. In the wake of the spill, BP CEO Tony Hayward launched a public relations campaign to 'win the hearts and minds' of the people.[9] A predictable apologist on Fox News claimed that natural seepage puts more oil into the ocean than accidents, and radio talk show host Rush Limbaugh assured his audience that oil is 'as natural as the ocean water'.[10] The *New York Times* reminded its readers that 'America needs the oil'.[11] All bring to mind what John Kenneth Galbraith once called 'the effort to make pollution seem palatable or worth the cost'. [12]

But the truth soon swamped these efforts. Each day brought new revelations about the magnitude of the disaster. Even Fox News reported that it 'could be much worse than we knew'.[13] Experts estimated the rupture at 40,000–100,000 barrels per day, far above BP's claim of 5,000 barrels.[14] 'It is clear BP has been lying,' concluded Congressman Ed Markey, chairman of the House Subcommittee on Energy and the Environment.[15]

The bad news about fossil fuels is not limited to the Gulf of Mexico. 'All oil comes from someone's backyard,' observes Lisa Margonelli in the *New York Times*, noting that 'Nigeria has suffered spills equivalent to that of the Exxon Valdez every year since 1969'.[16] Mine disasters from West Virginia to Russia and China underscore the real costs of coal.[17] The extraction of Canadian tar sands, now the most important source of US oil imports, is chopping into the world's largest boreal forest and creating sludge ponds 'so toxic that the companies try to frighten birds away with scarecrows and propane cannons'.[18]

In the best-case scenario – with no accidents and minimal environmental damage from extraction – burning fossil fuels 'only' emits greenhouse gases that threaten future generations, along with co-pollutants that cause roughly 20,000 premature deaths annually in the United States.[19]

As the real costs of fossil fuels become more apparent, support grows for the clean energy transition. 'The disaster in the Gulf only underscores that even as we pursue domestic production to reduce our reliance on imported oil,' President Obama declared in the wake of the spill, 'our long-term security depends on the development of alternative sources of fuel and new transportation technologies.'[20] If the Gulf disaster helps to accelerate this transition, it will not have been entirely in vain.

Chapter 21

FOUR PILLARS OF CLIMATE JUSTICE

Climate justice is not only a moral imperative – it is a political necessity.

It is time for a new strategy for climate policy in America – a strategy founded on climate justice.

Climate justice has four pillars:

- *Action:* Climate change will affect us all, but its heaviest costs will fall upon low-income people who live closest to the margin of survival and are least able to afford air conditioners, sea walls and other types of insurance. Climate inaction is climate injustice.
- *Adaptation for all:* We cannot prevent climate change altogether. Investments in adaptation are necessary, but how should these be allocated? The conventional economists' prescription is that investments should be guided by 'willingness to pay', which of course depends on ability to pay. The implications of this logic were spelled out two decades ago in the Summers memorandum that purported to make the case for dumping toxic waste in low-wage countries.[1] Climate justice requires that investment in adaptation should be guided by human needs, not by the distribution of purchasing power.
- *Co-benefits:* Burning fossil fuel releases not only carbon dioxide but also co-pollutants that endanger human health. Co-pollutant damages per ton of carbon dioxide vary greatly, so it makes sense to reduce emissions where the benefits of co-pollutant reductions are biggest. Because co-pollutants disproportionately impact low-income communities and minorities, integrating them into climate policy is a matter of climate justice as well as efficiency.[2]
- *Dividends:* A cap on carbon emissions is essential, but instead of giving free permits to polluters – a central plank in 'cap-and-trade' schemes – polluters should pay. Permits are valuable: their holders will receive the fossil fuel price increases triggered by the cap. They should be auctioned, not given away, eliminating any need for permit trading. The revenues should be returned to the people as the rightful owners of the atmosphere's limited carbon-absorptive capacity (or any country's share of it).

Climate justice has not been the centerpiece of climate policy initiatives the United States. All too often, what is right has been subordinated to what is deemed politically expedient. Ironically, however, the proponents of *realpolitik* have been guilty of wishful thinking.

Nowhere was this more visible than in the cap-and-trade proposals that repeatedly went down to defeat in Washington in the first decade of this century. Any strategy that keeps fossil fuels in the ground by restricting their supply (as opposed to decreasing demand for them) inevitably will raise their price. The question is, Who will get the money? Cap-and-trade was based on a political calculation: give free permits to corporate polluters to clear the way for passage of a climate bill. But in the end, the polluters preferred no bill at all.

Instead of courting the fossil fuel lobby, a climate justice policy would turn to the people for political support. It would appeal to their economic interests and just as importantly to their moral values. When they enter the ballot box, voters think about not only what is in their interest but also what is right. When the two are aligned, public opinion becomes a potent force.

In passing legislation, politicians typically rely more on support from lobbyists than from the people. But in the case of climate policy, business-as-usual politics has reached a dead end. The time has come for a bold departure. Today climate justice is more than a moral imperative: it is a political necessity.

Chapter 22

THE PERVERSE LOGIC OF OFFSETS

Greenhouse gas offsets in the Kyoto Protocol's Clean Development Mechanism created perverse incentives to pollute more.

A little-known greenhouse gas called HFC-23 made the news in 2012. Also called fluoroform, it's a waste gas generated in the manufacture of refrigerants. Compared to carbon dioxide (CO_2), HFC-23 is a minor greenhouse gas because the quantities emitted are small. Pound-for-pound, however, it traps more than 10,000 times as much heat.

The UN's Clean Development Mechanism (CDM), set up under the Kyoto Protocol as a way for industrialized countries to 'offset' their own CO_2 emissions by paying for comparable actions in developing countries, counts destruction of one pound of HFC-23 as equivalent to prevention of 11,700 pounds of CO_2 emissions.

The CDM pays large sums to coolant manufacturers in India, China and elsewhere to destroy the HFC-23 they produce. Indeed, these payments became the largest single item in the CDM budget: in 2012, HFC-23 disposal got 50 per cent more CDM money than wind power and 100 times more than solar energy.

The rub is that paying firms not to pollute gives rise to a perverse incentive. A firm that threatens to pollute more gets paid more. Manufacturers upped their production of the refrigerants (which are themselves greenhouse gases, too, albeit less potent ones), in order to produce more HFC-23 as a byproduct, so they then can get paid to destroy it.

It's a great example of what economists E. K. Hunt and Ralph d'Arge once called capitalism's 'invisible foot': when polluters are paid to clean up pollution, they create more of it, guided by an evil twin of Adam Smith's invisible hand.[1] Some firms made half their total profits from HFC-23 disposal payments.[2]

People living near the coolant factories didn't do as well. In the state of Gujarat in western India, residents of an adjacent village complained of skin rashes, birth defects and damages to crops caused by a noxious fog that burns the eyes and lungs.[3]

When the European Union halted further HFC-23 payments, firms responded by threatening to release the gas into the atmosphere. A scientist at the Environmental Investigation Agency, which opposes the pollution subsidies, put the matter bluntly: 'Attempting to force countries into squandering billions on fake offsets that actually increase production of greenhouse gases,' he said, 'is extortion.'[4]

The HFC-23 fiasco offers three crucial lessons for climate policy.

Lesson number one: *Don't pay polluters.* Instead, make polluters pay. Putting a price on pollution via carbon taxes or auctioned permits – while also controlling emissions by means of conventional regulation – can be a good idea. But how good depends on who pays whom. When polluters pay to pollute, they have an incentive to cut emissions above and beyond what's mandated by existing regulations. Furthermore, the payments establish the core principle that the waste-absorption capacity of the atmosphere is not an unlimited resource that polluters can use free of charge but rather a scarce resource that belongs to us all. In keeping with the principle of common ownership, pollution payments should be returned to the people via green dividends and investments in public goods.

Lesson number two: *No offsets.* A major problem with offsets, as the HFC-23 fiasco illustrates, is that it can be difficult or impossible to ensure that they cut emissions below what would have occurred in their absence – an issue known as 'additionality'. There are compelling reasons, both practical and moral, for industrialized countries to help developing countries to reduce greenhouse gas emissions. But this assistance should come on top of acting to cut their own emissions at home, not via offsets as a substitute for doing so.

Lesson number three: *Watch co-pollutants.* Emissions of greenhouse gases often go together with emissions of toxic co-pollutants that harm nearby communities. The magnitude of air-quality impacts varies from polluter to polluter, depending among other things on investments in pollution control. 'The accounting logic in the UN system is that one ton of CO_2 removed in Gujarat is the same as one ton in New York,' notes economist Siddhartha Dabhi of the University of Essex, 'but that doesn't consider local effects.'[5] Climate policy should consider the local effects of co-pollutants and be designed with an eye on securing health benefits, particularly in the locations with the heaviest pollution burdens.

If policymakers manage to learn these lessons, those perverse HFC-23 payments will not have been entirely counterproductive.

Chapter 23

CLIMATE POLICY AS WEALTH CREATION

Returning carbon revenues to the public as dividends would embody the principle that we all own Earth's resources in equal and common measure. Excerpted from a lecture presented at the University of Pittsburgh in March 2014.

Broadly speaking, there are two types of policies to reduce carbon emissions from fossil-fuel combustion. One set of policies operates on the demand side of the picture to reduce our need for fossil fuels. These include investments in energy efficiency, mass transit and alternative sources of energy – investments that result in lower demand for fossil fuels at any given price.

The other set of policies operates on the supply side. These policies increase the price of fossil fuels by putting a tax on carbon emissions or, alternatively, by putting a cap the amount of fossil fuels we use and hence on emissions. The result is similar to what happens when OPEC restricts supply in order to increase the price of oil.

Why Climate Policies on the Supply Side?

Policies that aim to shift demand – via investments in mass transit, clean and renewable energy, or energy efficiency – often take time, maybe even decades, to be implemented fully. If we want to see significant reductions in fossil-fuel use in the short run, we need policies that operate on the price and reduce consumption today. This is one reason why I think that price-based policies ought to be part of the policy mix.

In addition, price-based policies themselves can be critical in reducing demand over the longer run. When consumers, households, firms and public-sector institutions know that over the next decade or two the price of fossil fuels will rise inexorably due to policies that curtail supply, they will have a powerful incentive to make investments in energy efficiency and renewable energy sources. They will face price signals that push that investment forward.

The easiest way to put a price on carbon emissions is through an upstream system, which means that you apply the price where the carbon enters the economy, not where it comes out the smokestack or tailpipe. So that means at the tanker terminals, the pipelines and the coal-mine heads. The Congressional Budget Office estimates than an upstream system would involve about 2,000 'compliance entities' – that's the name for the folks who have to pay the tax or surrender a permit for each ton of carbon that they bring into the economy.[1] When the carbon price is charged upstream, it becomes part of the price of the fuel and this is passed along to businesses and consumers, just as OPEC supply restrictions raise fuel prices at the pump. This creates incentives to reduce consumption in the short run and for investments that will reduce emissions over the longer haul.

There are two instruments that we can use to price carbon. One is a tax, the other is a cap. A tax sets the price and allows the quantity of emissions to fluctuate. A cap sets the quantity and allows the price of emissions to fluctuate. Apart from this difference, they are basically the same thing. You can think of them both as involving permits. A tax says, 'Here are permits, as long as you pay the price we've set for them, you can have as many as you want.' A cap says, 'Here is a fixed number of permits, and we're going to let their price be determined at an auction or in a market.'

Since the central policy objective is to hit the quantity target – to reduce the quantity of emissions to the desired level – it seems to me that targeting the quantity directly, rather than the price, makes a lot of sense. We do not know exactly what relationship will hold between quantity and price. For instance, we may have evidence that in past years a 10 per cent increase in the price of transportation fuels resulted on average in a 3 per cent reduction in demand for them in the short run, but that relationship is not precise because different episodes yield differing results. Moreover, the responsiveness of demand to price can change over time, particularly as new technologies are discovered. So if you want to meet the quantity target, setting a cap has some advantages over setting a tax.

One way or another, however, what is important is to get a price on carbon. When we put a price on carbon, what we're doing is moving from an *open-access* regime – a situation where there are no property rights – to create new property rights. Regulations already assert a certain type of property right, the right of the public acting through the government to set rules about how resources are used. Putting a price on emissions takes this one step further. It not only sets rules about using the resource but also charges a price for using it. So it moves further along the spectrum from a complete absence of property rights towards a fuller set of property rights.

How Much Will It Cost?

Back in 2009, the Speaker of the House of Representatives, John Boehner, claimed in the debate on the American Clean Energy and Security Act – known as the Waxman-Markey bill, after its Democratic co-sponsors, Henry Waxman and Ed Markey – that its cap-and-trade system for carbon emissions would 'drive up the prices for food, gasoline and electricity'. His fellow Republican Congressman Mike Pence declared that it would be 'the largest tax increase in American history'.[2] Notwithstanding the political hyperbole, the Republican critics were not entirely wrong. A cap on carbon emissions *would* be like a tax increase, and it *would* be substantial. It has to be substantial if it is going to bring about the changes in consumption of fossil fuels that are needed to push forward the clean-energy transition. We are talking about big changes, something on the order of an 80 per cent reduction in emissions by the year 2050. We are talking about an energy revolution. The kinds of price increases that would be ultimately needed to drive it forward are not inconsequential.

What was the Democratic response? 'No, no, it's not a tax. It's not a big price increase, it's really not going to hurt people all that much. Why, the cost to the average American is only equivalent to a postage stamp a day.' But this postage-stamp-a-day price tag was an estimate of something quite different from the price increases that households would face. It was the estimated cost of abatement – the cost of investments to reduce fossil fuel consumption. That cost would not have been huge in the early stages of the policy, because there is a lot of low-hanging fruit in terms of abatement opportunities.

The consulting firm McKinsey & Co. has found that some investments even would have a *negative* cost.[3] In other words, if you make those investments to reduce carbon emissions, you actually get money back because it is so efficient. So overall, you can achieve reductions at a fairly modest cost. But the money spent on reducing emissions is not the same as the price paid on the emissions we are not reducing.

That is the higher price that consumers will be paying for their use of fossil fuels, and that is the primary reason for the price increases you will see at every gas pump, on every electric bill, and that you will see trickling through into the prices of other commodities in proportion to the use of fossil fuels in their production and distribution.

Gasoline prices are the most politically visible prices in America. They are advertised in 12-inch high numbers on street corners across the country. During the 2008 Presidential campaign, when all the major candidates – including Hillary Clinton and John McCain – were talking about global warming and said they were in favor of limiting carbon emissions with a cap-and-trade policy, gasoline prices happened to go up. And both Clinton and McCain said this was a terrible burden on the American people, and called for a federal gas tax holiday to relieve this burden.[4] Well, the federal gasoline tax is about 18 cents a gallon – it's really not that much. Compared to the price increases that we're going to see if we have a serious climate policy, I hate to tell it to you folks, but 18 cents rounds to about zero.

We could see gas prices going well above $5 a gallon in the first few years of a serious policy and ultimately higher than that. How are you going to have a policy that squares the circle between, on the one hand, the need to price those emissions in order to combat climate change, and on the other hand, even those politicians who see climate change as a problem saying that we can't let the price of gas go up because it's going to hurt American families?

Who Gets the Money?

Over the decades needed for the clean energy transition, we could be talking about trillions of dollars in the extra money paid for fossil fuels as a result of policies that curtail their supply. The question is: Who will get the money? To put it differently, who owns the atmosphere?

One possible answer is the fossil fuel corporations. We could allow them to keep the money that consumers pay in higher prices. If we give free permits to the firms (up to the limit set by a cap) on the basis of some allocation formula, prices to consumers go up and the recipients of free permits get the money. Such permits would be tradable, as firms that want more permits would buy them from others that prefer to sell. This is the origin of the phrase 'cap and trade', which really means 'cap *and giveaway* and trade', since if you don't give away the permits for free, there is no need for them to be tradable.

Who ultimately would receive the resulting windfall profits? The money would go to whoever owns the firms in proportion to stock ownership. Since stock ownership is very unequal, most would go to people at the top of the wealth pyramid. Some of the money would flow abroad, too, to foreign owners.

A second possibility is 'cap and spend'. In this case cap, the government doesn't give away the permits but instead auctions them monthly or quarterly. Only so many permits are on the table, and the firms that want to bring carbon into the economy bid for them. The revenue from permit auctions (or the carbon tax) is retained by the government, and it can be used to increase government spending on anything: on public education, on environmental improvements, on foreign wars, you name it. Alternatively, it could be used to cut taxes or reduce the deficit. All of these are possible uses for revenue under a cap-and-spend policy.

The third possibility is 'cap and dividend' (called 'fee and dividend' in the case of a carbon tax). In this policy, the money is recycled to the people on an equal per capita basis. Again, permits are auctioned (or the tax is collected), but every month or every quarter the money is paid out equally to all. This protects the purchasing power of working families and thereby helps to build durable public support for the policy over the decades it will take to complete the clean-energy transition.

How Would Carbon Dividends Work?

A carbon price is a regressive tax: it hits the poor harder than the rich as a proportion of their household incomes. Because fuels are a necessity, not a luxury, they account for a bigger share of the family budget in low-income families than in middle-income families, and a bigger share in middle-income families than in high-income families. As you move up the income scale, however, you have a bigger carbon footprint – you tend to consume more fuels and more things that are produced and distributed using fuels. More affluent people consume more of just about everything. So in absolute dollar terms, when you price carbon, high-income folks will pay more than low-income folks.

The purchasing power of households is eroded as the carbon price is passed through to them in the form of price increases for fuels and other goods and services. But with cap and dividend, money also comes back to them. Those with outsized carbon footprints pay more in higher prices than they receive in dividends; those who consume less receive more than they pay. Because expenditures are skewed to the wealthy, most people *would get back more than they pay* under such a policy. As gasoline prices rise at the pump, then, most people will say, 'I don't mind because I'm getting my share back in a fair and very visible way.' It is politically fantastical, I believe, to imagine that there will be durable public support for a climate policy that substantially increases energy prices in any other way.

There are precedents for doing this kind of thing. The best known is the Alaska Permanent Fund, established when North Slope oil production was starting up. The voters decided that the oil belongs to every Alaskan in equal and common measure – current Alaskans and future generations, too. So the state charges a royalty or severance tax for every barrel of oil, puts the money in the Fund, and uses it in three ways. Part goes for long-term public investment. Part goes into financial assets, so that the Fund will be there, even after the oil is gone, for future Alaskans. And part is paid out in equal per-person dividends to every man, woman and child in the state of Alaska. That payment has been as much as $2,000 a year. Paying dividends to the people is not a complicated thing to do. It's not rocket science. It's dead easy.

Apart from helping to support family incomes, I believe that the dividend policy has deep philosophical appeal. It is founded on the principle that we all own Earth's resources, the gifts of nature, in equal and common measure. The planet's limited capacity to absorb carbon emissions does not belong to corporations. It does not belong to governments. It belongs to all of us. The carbon dividend is a way of implementing that common ownership rather than abdicating ownership and giving our resources away for free.

Ask people, not only in this country but around the world, 'Who owns the air? Who owns the gifts of nature?' The answer you will hear most often is that we all own them together. Our challenge in addressing climate change is to translate this widely shared principle into actual policy by which, as the owners of these gifts, we use them responsibly. In the case of the biosphere's ability to absorb carbon dioxide emissions, that means limiting the amount we put in the atmosphere. That is what we need to do.

Chapter 24

THE CARBON DIVIDEND

The climate bill proposed in 2014 by Congressman Chris Van Hollen would auction carbon permits and return 100 per cent of the money straight to the American people as equal dividends.

From the scorched earth of climate debates a bold idea is rising – one that just might succeed in breaking the nation's current political impasse on reducing carbon emissions. That's because it would bring tangible gains for American families here and now.

A major obstacle to climate policy in the United States has been the perception that the government is telling us how to live today in the name of those who will live tomorrow. Present-day pain for future gain is never an easy sell. And many Americans have a deep aversion to anything that smells like bigger government.

What if we could find a way to put more money in the pockets of families and less carbon in the atmosphere without expanding government? If the combination sounds too good to be true, read on.

Representative Chris Van Hollen, Democrat of Maryland, introduced legislation that would require coal, oil and natural gas companies to buy a permit for each ton of carbon in the fuels they sell.[1] Permits would be auctioned, and 100 per cent of the proceeds would be returned straight to the American people as equal dividends.

Paying dividends to all isn't rocket science. The state of Alaska has been doing it since 1982. That's when the Alaska Permanent Fund, the brainchild of Governor Jay S. Hammond, a Republican, began to pay dividends from oil royalties based on the principle that the state's natural wealth belongs to all its people. Residents claim their dividends by filling out an online form. Not surprisingly, the Alaska Permanent Fund is permanently popular among Alaskans. From 1982 through 2009, the fund paid out $17.5 billion. The biggest payout, by the way, came under Governor Sarah Palin.

The main difference between Alaska's fund and the one Mr Van Hollen has proposed is that instead of creating an incentive to pump more oil, his legislation creates an incentive to burn less oil and other carbon-based fuels.

The number of permits initially would be capped at the level of our 2005 carbon dioxide emissions. This cap would gradually ratchet down to 80 per cent below that level by 2050. Prices of fossil fuels would rise as the cap tightens, spurring private investment in energy efficiency and clean energy. Energy companies would pass the cost of permits to consumers in the form of higher fuel prices. But for most families, the gain in carbon dividends would be greater than the pain. In fact, my calculations show that more than 80 per cent of American households would come out ahead financially – and that doesn't even count the benefits of cleaner air and a cooler planet.

As the cap tightens, prices of fossil fuels would rise faster than quantity would fall, so total revenues would rise. The tighter the cap, the bigger the dividend. Voters not only would want to keep the policy in place for the duration of the clean energy transition, they also would want to strengthen it.

The net effect on any household would depend on its carbon footprint – how much it spends, directly and indirectly, on fossil fuels. The less carbon it consumes, the bigger its net benefit. But why would a vast majority emerge as winners?

There are two reasons. First, among final consumers, households account for about two-thirds of fossil fuel use in the United States. Most of the remainder is consumed by government. In Mr Van Hollen's bill, households would receive these other carbon dollars, too.

Republicans should welcome this feature, since over the years it would return billions of dollars from the government to the people. Unlike a carbon tax or permit sales that bring in more revenue for the government, Mr Van Hollen's bill is, in effect, a tax cut.

The second reason is the dramatic skew in household incomes. The outsize consumption – and outsize carbon footprints – of the richest 10 per cent of Americans means that they'll furnish a similarly high fraction of the carbon dollars generated by household spending on gasoline, electricity, airplane trips and so on. For these households, the dividends won't outweigh the costs. But the affluent can afford to pay for their emissions.

Does this bill stand a snowball's chance in the partisan hell of Washington?

Its main political weakness is that no one stands to make a killing on it. The bill's main strength is that it protects the incomes of ordinary Americans as it protects the planet for their grandchildren.

In a democracy, this outcome is not too good to be true. If any climate policy can win bipartisan support, this is it. But it will succeed only if the American people – in blue states, red states and everywhere in between – come together to make their representatives act.

Chapter 25

KEEPING THE GOVERNMENT WHOLE*

Carbon pricing will raise costs for governments, but policies can be designed to maintain their purchasing power along with the incentive to reduce their carbon footprints.

If and when the United States puts a cap or tax on carbon emissions as part of the effort to address global climate change, this will increase the prices of fossil fuels, significantly impacting not only household consumers but also local, state and federal governments. Households can be 'made whole', in the sense that whatever amount the public pays in higher fuel prices is recycled to the public, by means of a carbon dividend policy. Individual households will come out ahead or behind in monetary terms depending on whether they consume below-average or above-average amounts of carbon. Here we consider policy options for 'keeping the government whole', too, policies to ensure that additional revenues to government compensate adequately for the additional costs that result from the carbon price.

The price impacts of a carbon cap will be felt by federal, state and local governments. The prices of heating oil and coal-fired electricity will rise for schools and other public buildings, just as they will rise for homeowners. The prices of gasoline and diesel will rise for the Pentagon and other government agencies, just as they will for private citizens. To keep the government whole – to maintain real government spending and services at current levels – government revenues would need to grow correspondingly.

In this chapter we analyse two policy options for keeping the government whole:

- *Distribute 100 per cent of revenue to individuals as taxable dividends:* Here we assume that dividends are subject to federal and state income taxes at the same rate as ordinary income and also that dividends are spent by households and hence subject to state sales tax. We find that 24 per cent of dividends (on average) would be returned to the federal and state governments, an

---

* Co-authored with Matthew Riddle.

amount sufficient to keep the government whole in that it compensates for the impact of higher fossil fuel prices on government purchasing power.
* *Revenue set aside for government, coupled with tax-free dividends to individuals:* An alternative policy option is to earmark a fraction of the carbon revenue (that is, the revenue from carbon taxes or the sale of carbon permits) for governments, rather than recycling 100 per cent of it to the public. In this option, dividends to individuals are treated as tax-free. To facilitate comparison between the two options, we assume that the set-aside is calibrated to keep the government share of total carbon revenue the same as under the first option.

We examine the distributional impacts of both policies by dividing the US population into 10 deciles, ranked from poorest to richest on the basis of per capita expenditure. Our calculations are based on a permit price of $200 per ton of carbon (about $55 per ton of carbon dioxide), a price that would yield annual carbon revenues of roughly $300 billion/year.

What will happen as the carbon price rises in successive years, moving towards greater emissions reductions? As the quantity of emissions falls, their price will rise. If past experience is a guide, the percentage increase in prices is likely to be larger than the percentage decrease in quantity (because demand for fossil fuels is price-inelastic), so total carbon revenue will rise, too. This will increase the magnitude of the distributional effects reported below, but will not change their pattern.

Government Carbon Consumption

What share of revenue from the sale of carbon permits would be required to keep government whole, that is, to offset the effects of carbon prices on the balance between government expenditures and government revenues, with 'government' here taken to encompass federal, state and local governments?

The most evident effect on government of any policy that puts a price on carbon emissions is to raise the cost of government's own consumption of fossil fuels and everything that uses fossil fuels in its production and distribution. Table 25.1 presents estimates of government carbon consumption, based on input-output data on the fossil fuel content of the various categories of expenditures. Government expenditure accounts for about 14.5 per cent of the nation's 'carbon footprint'.[1] State and local government account for 10.8 per cent and federal government for 3.6 per cent. These percentages are smaller than their shares in total expenditure: the carbon intensity of public expenditure is less than that of private consumption, reflecting the higher proportion of services in government consumption.

In addition to the impact of increased costs due to higher fossil fuel prices, the introduction of carbon permits could have indirect impacts on the balance

Table 25.1 Government and private shares of US carbon emissions (2002)

Sector	Share of expenditure (%)	Carbon intensity (kg CO_2/$)	Share of emissions (%)
Government: Total	19.0	0.43	14.5
Federal government	6.5	0.31	3.6
Defence	4.2	0.31	2.3
Other	2.3	0.32	1.3
State and local government	12.5	0.49	10.8
Education	5.4	0.48	4.6
Other	7.1	0.50	6.2
Private: Total	72.4	0.57	73.5
Household consumption	64.6	0.57	65.7
Non-profit institutions	7.7	0.57	7.8
Exports	8.8	0.78	12.0

Sources: Authors' calculations. For details, see James K. Boyce and Matthew Riddle, 'Keeping the Government Whole'. Amherst, MA: Political Economy Research Institute, Working Paper No. 188, November 2008.

between government expenditure and revenue. These include increases in government transfer payments (for example, Social Security benefits and federal pensions) that are indexed to prices, and reduced personal income tax collections if no change were made to the indexing of exemptions and tax brackets. It has been estimated that each of these could have impacts roughly equivalent to a further 7 per cent of carbon revenue.[2] If so, adding these to the direct effects of higher fuel prices on government purchasing power would mean that roughly 28 per cent of total carbon revenues will be needed to keep the government whole. These indirect impacts could be offset, however, by the recycling of carbon revenue to the public under a carbon dividend policy. Payment of equal per capita dividends acts as a substitute for indexing transfer payments in response to policy-induced fuel price increases, as both are intended to insulate households from the impact of the price increases on their real incomes. And if the dividends are treated as taxable income, this will augment tax revenues.

Allocating Carbon Revenue among Federal, State and Local Governments

Whatever fraction of total carbon revenue is recycled to government, a key issue will be how to allocate this money among federal, state and local governments. This is particularly important in the case of local governments, which often do not levy income taxes or sales taxes and hence lack automatic mechanisms to obtain revenues under a carbon dividend policy.

There are two stages to this problem. The first is how to allocate carbon revenues across the three levels of government: federal, state and local. The second is how to allocate revenues among the 50 states and, within states, among local governments.

With regard to the first stage, one possible rule is to apportion the government share of carbon revenue across the three levels of government in proportion to their respective expenditures on goods and services. Based on the expenditure shares reported in Table 25.1, this would translate into roughly 34 per cent of the government carbon-revenue pool being allocated to the federal government, and the remaining 66 per cent to state and local governments. This does not take into account differences in the carbon intensity of expenditure across the three levels of government. As shown in the table, state and local government expenditures tend to be more carbon-intensive than federal expenditures. An alternative rule is to apportion carbon revenue across the three levels of government in proportion to their carbon emissions, that is, in proportion to the extent to which the carbon price will raise their operating costs. Under this formula, the federal share of government carbon revenue would be 24 per cent and the state and local share would be 76 per cent.

With regard to the second-stage problem – allocation across the 50 states and across local governments within states – any revenue-sharing rule should maintain incentives for governments themselves to improve their energy efficiency and invest in clean energy. In the same way that a carbon dividend policy creates incentives for consumers and private-sector firms to reduce their use of fossil fuels, state and local governments should be given incentives to do the same. This implies that interstate and inter-locality revenue allocation should not simply be based on carbon use. One possible rule is to allocate revenue on the basis of population – that is, on an equal per capita basis – a formula that would be consistent with the logic of distributing dividends to households on an equal per capita basis.

Option #1: Distribute 100 Per Cent of the Carbon Revenue as Taxable Dividends

One option is to recycle all of the carbon revenue to households as individual dividends. With a carbon permit price of $200/ton carbon, the dividends would amount to $1161/person/year. Assuming this is treated as ordinary income, we estimate that 24.2 per cent of dividend payments would return to government in the form of income taxes and sales taxes. Federal income taxes account for 18.1 per cent of this amount; state income and sales taxes account for the remainder.[3] Tax rates vary by income class, and we estimate that the share of dividends claimed by taxes would range from 10.2 per cent in the poorest decile to 39.7 per cent in the top decile.

The net distributional impact of this option is shown in Table 25.2. Because any carbon pricing policy charges households (via higher prices for fossil fuels) in proportion to their carbon consumption, higher-expenditure households generally pay more than lower-expenditure households. Richer households pay more than they receive in dividends, while poorer households receive more than they pay.

The bottom seven deciles come out ahead, in the sense that their dividends exceed what they pay as a result of higher fuel prices. The 'winners' – here defined in purely monetary terms, without adding the benefits from curbing global warming – outnumber the 'losers' by roughly a 2:1 margin. There are two reasons for this. First, expenditure is skewed to the top of the income distribution. Second, the after-tax share of total carbon revenues retained by households (75.8%) is greater than the household share of carbon emissions and hence carbon charges (65.7%, as shown in Table 25.1).

At the same time, the government share of carbon revenue that is recouped via taxes on dividends (24.2%) exceeds the government share of carbon emissions (14.5%). Indeed, it does so by a margin that is large enough to compensate for at least some of the effects of indexation of transfer payments and tax brackets on government revenue (if these are not addressed via other policies) and/or to fund public investments that complement the carbon pricing policy by supporting the clean energy transition. In other words, the taxable dividend option would keep the government whole.[4]

Option #2: Revenue Set Aside for Government Coupled with Tax-Free Dividends to Individuals

A second option is to set aside enough carbon revenue for government to offset the policy's impact on government expenditure, returning the remainder to the public as tax-free dividends. To facilitate comparison between the two options, in our calculations we assume that government again receives 24.2 per cent of the total carbon revenue (primarily via the revenue that is set aside, with a small amount also coming from sales taxes when households spend their dividends).

The net distributional impact is shown in Table 25.3. Under this option, the bottom seven deciles again come out ahead financially. The net gains for the lower deciles are somewhat lower than under the first option, however, as are the net costs for the upper deciles. The distributional incidence therefore is somewhat less progressive. The difference arises from how the government share of carbon revenue is financed. In the previous option, the fraction of

Table 25.2 Distributional impact of cap-and-dividend policy with 100 per cent of revenue paid as taxable dividends

Decile (based on per capita expenditure)	Expenditure per capita	Charge (costs from higher fossil fuel prices) per capita	Dividend per capita	Taxes (federal + state) on dividends (%)	Taxes (federal + state) on dividends ($)	Net impact ($)	Net impact (as % of expenditure)
1	1927	269	1161	10.2	119	773	40.1
2	3521	405	1161	10.8	125	631	17.9
3	4736	493	1161	17.6	205	464	9.8
4	5991	589	1161	21.2	246	326	5.4
5	7380	653	1161	25.1	291	217	2.9
6	8847	732	1161	26.4	306	123	1.4
7	10711	823	1161	26.6	309	30	0.3
8	13228	938	1161	28.2	328	-104	-0.8
9	17178	1139	1161	36.5	424	-402	-2.3
10	29943	1639	1161	39.7	460	-938	-3.1
Average	10346	768	1161	24.2	281	112	1.1

Sources: Authors' calculations. For details, see James K. Boyce and Matthew Riddle, 'Keeping the Government Whole'. Amherst, MA: Political Economy Research Institute, Working Paper No. 188, November 2008.

Table 25.3 Distributional impact of cap-and-dividend policy with revenue set aside for government

Decile (based on per capita expenditure)	Expenditure per capita	Charge (costs from higher fossil fuel prices) per capita	Dividend per capita	Taxes (federal + state) on dividends (%)	Taxes (federal + state) on dividends ($)	Net impact ($)	Net impact (as % of expenditure)
1	1927	254	919	4.4	40	624	32.4
2	3521	390	919	4.4	40	488	13.9
3	4736	486	919	4.4	40	393	8.3
4	5991	586	919	4.4	40	293	4.9
5	7380	654	919	4.4	40	225	3.0
6	8847	733	919	4.4	40	145	1.6
7	10711	825	919	4.4	40	54	0.5
8	13228	941	919	4.4	40	-62	-0.5
9	17178	1149	919	4.4	40	-270	-1.6
10	29943	1649	919	4.4	40	-770	-2.6
Average	10346	767	919	4.4	40	112	1.1

Sources: Authors' calculations. For details, see James K. Boyce and Matthew Riddle, 'Keeping the Government Whole'. Amherst, MA: Political Economy Research Institute, Working Paper No. 188, November 2008.

dividends that is returned to government via taxes varies across the deciles, with a higher fraction coming from the more affluent households. In the second scenario, each person's dividend is reduced by exactly the same dollar amount – a policy that is, in effect, equivalent to a head tax.

Conclusions

This chapter has compared the distributional impacts of two alternative policies: distributing all of the carbon revenue to households as taxable dividends, or setting aside part of the carbon revenue for government while distributing the remainder to the public tax-free dividends. Both policies would protect the real incomes of the majority of American households, and both would have a progressive impact on the distribution of income, although the policy of recycling 100 per cent of carbon revenue to the public as taxable dividends has a stronger progressive impact.

Apart from recycling sufficient carbon revenue to government, a further issue is how to allocate this money among federal, state and local governments by means of a formula that is fair and at the same time maintains incentives for governments to curb their own emissions. We have suggested a two-step allocation rule for this purpose: first, apportion the revenue across the three levels of government – federal, state and local – according to their respective shares in GDP; and second, allocate revenue among states and local governments on the basis of population.

Any policy that increases the prices of fossil fuels will have significant impacts on all three levels of government as well as on consumers. This is true regardless of whether the price increase results from a tax or a cap, and in the case of a cap, regardless of whether permits are given away or auctioned to polluters. Higher prices are the corollary of scarcity, and scarcity (compared to what the situation would be without a carbon price) is precisely what the policy is intended to create.

Households can be made whole, in the sense that what the public at large pays in higher fuel prices is recycled back to the public, by a carbon dividend policy. Governments can be made whole, too, either by treating carbon dividends as taxable income or by earmarking some of the carbon revenue for government expenditure.

Chapter 26

AIR QUALITY CO-BENEFITS IN CLIMATE POLICY

Climate policy not only can benefit future generations: the here-and-now benefits of clean air are a compelling reason to phase out fossil fuels.

In addition to reducing emissions of carbon dioxide, policies that curtail the use of fossil fuels reduce emissions of many other air pollutants that harm human health, including particulate matter, sulfur dioxide, nitrogen oxides and carbon monoxide. In fact, some studies that have assigned monetary values to the damages from carbon dioxide and these 'co-pollutants' have put higher values on the latter. Co-pollutant intensity (the ratio of co-pollutant damages to carbon dioxide emissions) varies across emission sources, and for this reason the pattern of emissions reductions across locations and economic sectors is important for both efficiency and equity.

The World Health Organization characterizes air pollution as 'the world's largest single environmental health risk'. Outdoor air pollution is responsible worldwide for 3.7 million deaths annually.[1]

Valuing the Human Costs of Air Pollution

A multi-country analysis by the Organisation for Economic Co-operation and Development (OECD) concluded in 2014 that outdoor air pollution (specifically, particulate matter and ozone) was responsible for 2.45 million premature deaths annually in the OECD countries plus China and India (see Table 26.1). To monetize these impacts, the OECD multiplied the number of deaths by the 'value of a statistical life' (VSL), computed as a function of national income per capita, adding 10 per cent for the costs of non-fatal illnesses. The resulting total cost of human health effects of outdoor air pollution in these countries amounted to $3.5 trillion per year, with the OECD member countries accounting for about half and China and India for the rest.

Table 26.1 Costs of outdoor pollution in China, India and OECD countries

Country	Premature deaths (per year)	Value of a statistical life[1] (USD million)	Economic cost[2] (USD billion/ year)
China	1,278,890	0.975	1,371.4
India	692,425	0.602	458.4
US	110,292	4.498	545.8
Japan	65,776	3.068	222.0
Germany	42,578	3.480	163.0
Italy	34,143	2.995	112.5
Turkey	28,924	2.024	64.4
Poland	25,091	2.098	57.9
UK	24,064	3.554	94.1
Korea	23,161	3.027	77.1
Mexico	21,594	1.811	43.0
France	17,389	3.155	60.4
Other OECD	85,092	3.078	288.5
Total	**2,449,419**	**1.321**	**3,558.4**

Notes:

1 OECD calculation of the value of a statistical life (VSL) as a function of income per capita.
2 Economic cost = Costs of mortality + morbidity.

Source: OECD, *The Cost of Air Pollution: Health Impacts of Road Transport*. Paris, 2014. Tables 2.4, 2.7, 2.10 and 2.13–2.18.

In these calculations, the study used country-specific VSLs that place a lower value on air pollution deaths in India and China than in the wealthier OECD countries, offering the following rationale:

> *A VSL value is meant to be an aggregation of individual valuations: an aggregation of individuals' WTP [willingness to pay], as communicated through WTP surveys, to secure a marginal reduction in the risk of premature death. In the world as we know it, individuals are differently endowed with the means with which to make such a trade-off; some work for their living for a dollar a day, some inherit a fortune yielding unearned income of a billion dollars a year. Human societies without exception have sought to socialise these risks to a greater or lesser extent in the form of public goods [...] And it so happens that the level at which this socialisation of risks is executed today is the level of the nation-state. It is for this reason, and this reason alone, that it is appropriate to aggregate at the level of country-specific VSLs.[2]*

An alternative procedure would be to apply a uniform VSL to all countries, based on the premise that all human lives are equally valuable regardless of individual wealth or per capita income in the country where the person happens to reside, or to use a poverty-weighted VSL that puts greater value on the lives of the most vulnerable. Cass Sunstein remarks in his book, *Valuing Life*,

> *If poor people are subject to a risk of 1/10,000, they do not have less of a claim to public attention than wealthy people who are subject to exactly the same risk. In fact, they may have a greater claim, if only because they lack the resources to reduce that risk on their own.*[3]

Which of these valuation procedures is considered most appropriate may depend on who foots the bill for reducing health risks. When the poor must pay the cost of risk reduction themselves, a reasonable case can be made that they should not be expected or compelled to spend as much as wealthier people would spend for same protection. 'Requiring poor people to buy Volvos,' Sunstein remarks, 'is not the most sensible means of assisting them.' Whether this individual logic also applies to countries and their governments – with average per capita income replacing individual income – is not obvious, however. Sunstein himself warns that his argument 'should not be taken to support the ludicrous proposition that [international] donor institutions, both public and private, should value a risk reduction in a wealthy nation more than equivalent risk reduction in a poor nation'.[4]

Calculating the Co-pollutant Cost of Carbon

In addition to the burning of fossil fuels, air pollution comes from other sources including wildfires, the burning of biomass, and construction dust. The OECD's mortality data refer to deaths from all sources of outdoor air pollution, but in many countries fossil fuels are the most important source. Road transportation and electric power generation are estimated to account for more than half of premature mortality from outdoor air pollution in the United States, roughly one-third of the total in other OECD countries, and about one-fifth of the total in China and India, where residential and commercial energy use accounting for larger shares.[5] If we attribute virtually all air pollution from transportation and the power sector to fossil fuel combustion, plus one-quarter of the air pollution from other sectors, these figures would imply that fossil fuel use accounts for roughly 65 per cent of premature mortality from outdoor air pollution in the United States, 50 per cent in other OECD countries and 40 per cent in China and India.

Applying these percentages to the overall mortality data in Table 26.1, we can calculate health impacts of co-pollutants per ton carbon dioxide emissions. I term this ratio the co-pollutant cost of carbon (CPCC). Three measures of the CPCC are reported in Table 26.2. The first, the number

Table 26.2 Co-pollutant cost of carbon

Country	Premature deaths from fossil fuel emissions	CO_2 emissions (million mt)	Co-pollutant cost of carbon (per mt CO_2) Deaths US dollars		
			Deaths	OECD VSL	equal VSL
China	5,11,556	7,388.5	69.2	74.2	100.6
India	2,76,970	1,714.9	161.5	106.9	234.6
US	71,690	5,580.0	12.8	63.6	18.7
Japan	32,888	1,177.3	27.9	94.3	40.6
Germany	21,289	797.0	26.7	102.3	38.8
Italy	17,072	419.8	40.7	134.0	59.1
Turkey	14,462	268.5	53.9	119.9	78.2
Poland	12,546	304.6	41.2	95.0	59.0
UK	12,032	529.5	22.7	88.8	33.0
Korea	11,580	584.0	19.8	66.0	28.4
Mexico	10,797	434.0	24.9	49.6	35.6
France	8,694	385.6	22.5	78.3	32.3
Other OECD	42,546	2,588.3	16.4	55.7	23.6
Total	**1,044,122**	**22,172.1**	**47.1**	**68.4**	**68.4**

Sources: Premature deaths from fossil fuel emissions and co-pollutant cost of carbon: see text. CO_2 emissions from consumption of fossil fuels: US Energy Information Agency, https://www.eia.gov/cfapps/ipdbproject/IEDIndex3.cfm?tid=90&pid=44&aid=8, accessed on 11 February 2016.

of premature deaths per ton of carbon dioxide, ranges from fewer than 13 in the United States to more than 160 in India. The second, US dollars/ton using the OECD's mortality valuation method (in which VSL varies with per capita income), ranges from $50/ton in Mexico to $134/ton in Italy. The final measure applies a uniform VSL to all countries, while holding unchanged the sum total of monetary damages calculated in the OECD study. By this measure, which is directly proportional to deaths/ton, in India the CPCC exceeds $200/ton.

The CPCC for the United States in 2010 based on the OECD valuation procedure was $64/ton. If instead of the $4.5 million VSL used for deaths in the United States in the OECD study we were to apply the higher VSL used by the US Environmental Protection Agency (EPA), the CPCC would more than double.[6] It is instructive to compare this to the 'social cost of carbon' (SCC) used by the US government in regulatory analyses as a measure of climate damage from carbon dioxide emissions. The SCC does not include the damages from co-pollutants that are released along with carbon dioxide. The official SCC in 2015 ranged from $11 to $56/ton carbon dioxide depending on the choice of the discount rate, with a high-end figure of $105/ton used to test the sensitivity of cost-benefit analysis results to 'the potential for higher-than-average damages'.[7] In 2017, under the Trump administration the EPA lowered the SCC used for regulatory cost-benefit analysis to only $1-6/ton.[8] The CPCC in the United States thus is comparable to, or even larger than, the official SCC.

Other studies have come to similar conclusions. An analysis of prospective air quality co-benefits from 'deep decarbonization' in the United States found that it would prevent approximately 36,000 premature deaths/year from 2016 to 2030 and concluded that the monetary value of this public health benefit would surpass the climate benefits when the latter are valued on the basis of the official SCC.[9] In the European Union, a study by the Netherlands Environmental Assessment Agency concluded that the air quality co-benefits from a stringent climate policy would be large enough to offset the policy's costs 'even when the long-term benefits of avoided climate impacts are not taken into account'.[10]

For policymakers the salience of air quality co-benefits may be even greater than these monetary valuations suggest. Air quality benefits are predominantly near-term and national, whereas climate benefits are predominantly long-term and global. Greater attention to the magnitude of air quality co-benefits may therefore help to overcome the political impediments to climate policy that arise from myopia and concerns about international free riding.

Efficiency Implications

From an efficiency standpoint, two conclusions follow.

First, inclusion of the air quality co-benefits justifies tougher regulatory measures than if policy on burning fossil fuels were based solely on damages from carbon dioxide emissions. The full social cost of carbon – the sum of damages from both climate change and air pollution – provides a yardstick for higher carbon prices and more ambitious emission reduction targets.

Second, since air quality co-benefits per ton of carbon dioxide vary across pollution sources and locations, efficiency can be enhanced by designing policies so as to achieve deeper emissions reductions where co-benefits are higher. Consider the examples of a power plant located outside Bakersfield, California, and a petroleum refinery located in metropolitan Los Angeles, each of which emits about 3 million tons of carbon dioxide per year. The power plant emits about 50 tons of particulate matter and has fewer than 600 residents living in a 6-mile radius, while the refinery emits about 350 tons of particulates and has about 800,000 residents living within the same radius.[11]

Clearly, the health co-benefits brought about by a ton of carbon emission reductions will be greater at the refinery than at the power plant.

Equity Implications

From an equity standpoint as well, air quality co-benefits have important implications for the design of climate policy. In the United States, an executive order issued by President Bill Clinton in 1994 directs every US government agency to take steps to identify and rectify 'disproportionately high and adverse human health or environmental effects of its programmes, policies, and activities on minority populations and low-income populations'. Many US states now have similar environmental justice policies.[12]

The extent of disparities in air pollution exposure varies across facilities, industrial sectors and locations. For example, racial and ethnic minorities bear 59.5 per cent of the impact of particulate emissions from petroleum refineries in the United States, compared to 38.8 per cent in the case of power plants, the latter figure being much closer to their share in the national population.[13] An equity-sensitive climate policy would aim to achieve greater emissions reductions not only from those sources where air quality co-benefits are greater but also from sources where pollution damages are more unequally distributed by race, ethnicity and income.

Incorporating Air Quality Co-benefits into Climate Policy

Two broad categories of policy instruments can be used to reduce fossil-fuel combustion: regulations, such as fuel economy standards for automobiles and renewable portfolio standards for power plants; and price-based policies, such as a carbon tax or carbon permits. These two types of policies are not mutually exclusive. Anti-smoking policies, for example, combine restrictions on who can buy tobacco and where smoking is permitted with excise taxes to discourage smoking. Similarly, policies to cut sulfur dioxide emissions from power plants in the United States have combined mandated technologies and emission standards with a cap-and-trade permit system.

Unless and until one can reasonably assume that co-pollutant impacts are efficiently and equitably addressed by existing regulations, climate policy should take them into account. This approach is consistent with the growing embrace by policymakers of multi-pollutant strategies for air-quality management. For example, the authoritative US government document on regulatory impact analysis, Office of Management and Budget (OMB) Circular A-4, directs federal agencies to consider co-benefits (also known as 'ancillary benefits'):

Your analysis should look beyond the direct benefits and direct costs of your rulemaking and consider any important ancillary benefits and countervailing risks. An ancillary benefit is a favorable impact of the rule that is typically unrelated or secondary to the statutory purpose of the rulemaking (e.g., reduced refinery emissions due to more stringent fuel economy standards for light trucks).[14]

Air quality co-benefits can be incorporated into climate policy design in a variety of ways.

A minimalist option is simply to monitor co-pollutant emissions with a view to taking remedial measures if and when the climate policy has unacceptable impacts, such as exacerbation of environmental disparities across racial, ethnic or income groups. This was the strategy adopted in California's cap-and-trade programme for carbon emissions.

A more proactive option is to adopt a zone-based system for carbon pricing, with fewer carbon permits (or higher carbon taxes) in high-priority zones where greatest public health benefits will be obtained. Zone-specific caps were used, for example, in California's Regional Clean Air Incentives Market, initiated in 1994 to reduce emissions of sulfur dioxide and nitrogen oxides in the Los Angeles basin. Similarly, sector-specific permit or tax systems could be designed to ensure emissions reductions in those economic activities with the highest co-pollutant intensities or the most disproportionate impacts on minority and low-income populations.

A further step is to channel part of the revenue from carbon taxes or permit auctions into community benefit funds to protect public health and mitigate pollution impacts in vulnerable communities. This strategy has been used in California, too, where Senate Bill 535, signed into law in 2012, allocates 25 per cent of the revenue from the state's carbon permit auctions to projects that benefit disadvantaged communities.[15]

In sum, by incorporating air quality co-benefits into climate policy we can strengthen the case for the clean energy transition and at the same time advance the goals of efficiency and equity.

Chapter 27

CLIMATE ADAPTATION: PROTECTING MONEY OR PEOPLE?

Will climate adaptation be a commodity distributed on the basis of purchasing power or a human right for all?

At the December 2014 international climate talks in Lima, Peru, melting glaciers in the Andes and recent droughts provided a fitting backdrop for the negotiators' recognition that it is too late to prevent climate change altogether, no matter how fast we ultimately act to limit it. We now confront an issue that many once hoped to avoid: adaptation.

Adapting to climate change will carry a hefty price tag. Sea walls are needed to protect coastal areas against extreme floods, such as those in the New York area when Superstorm Sandy struck in 2012. We need early-warning and evacuation systems to protect against human tragedies, like those caused by Typhoon Haiyan in the Philippines in 2013 and by Hurricane Katrina in New Orleans in 2005.

Cooling centers and emergency services must be created to cope with heat waves, such as the one that killed 70,000 people in Europe in 2003. Water projects are needed to protect farmers and herders from extreme droughts, like the one that gripped the Horn of Africa in 2011. Large-scale replanting of forests with new species will be needed to keep pace as temperature gradients shift toward the poles.

Because adaptation won't come cheap, we must decide which investments are worth the cost.

A thought experiment illustrates the choices we face. Imagine that without major new investments in adaptation, climate change will cause world incomes to fall in the next two decades by 25 per cent across the board, with everyone's income going down, from the poorest farmworker in Bangladesh to the wealthiest real estate baron in Manhattan. Adaptation can cushion some but not all of these losses. What should be our priority: reduce losses for the farmworker or the property baron?

For the farmworker, and for a billion others in the world who subsist on about $1 a day, this 25 per cent income loss will be a disaster, perhaps spelling the difference between life and death. Yet, in dollars, the loss is just 25 cents a day.

For the real estate baron and other 'one-percenters' in the United States with average incomes of about $2,000 a day, the 25 per cent income loss would be a matter of regret, but not a threat to survival. They can manage to get by on $1,500 a day.

In human terms, the property baron's loss pales compared with that of the farmworker. But in dollar terms, it's 2,000 times larger.

Conventional economic models would prescribe spending more to protect the barons than the farmworkers of the world. The rationale was set forth with brutal clarity in a memorandum leaked in 1992 that was signed by Lawrence Summers, then chief economist of the World Bank. The memo asked whether the bank should encourage more migration of dirty industries to developing countries and concluded that 'the economic logic of dumping a load of toxic waste in the lowest-wage country is impeccable and we should face up to that'.[1] Climate change is just a new kind of toxic waste.

The 'economic logic' of the Summers memo – later said to have been penned tongue-in-cheek to provoke debate, which it certainly did – rests on a doctrine of 'efficiency' that counts all dollars equally. Whether it goes to a starving child or a millionaire, a dollar is a dollar. The task of economists, in this view, is to maximize the size of the total dollar pie. How it is sliced is not their problem.

A different way to set adaptation priorities is to count each person equally, not each dollar. This approach is founded on the ethical principle that a healthy environment is a human right, not a commodity to be distributed on the basis of purchasing power, nor a privilege to be distributed on the basis of political power.

This equity principle is widely embraced around the world, from the affirmation in the US Declaration of Independence that people have an inalienable right to 'life, liberty and the pursuit of happiness', to the guarantee in the South African Constitution that everyone has the right 'to an environment that is not harmful to their health or well-being'. It puts safeguarding the lives of the poor ahead of safeguarding the property of the rich.

In the years ahead, climate change will confront the world with hard choices: whether to protect as many dollars as possible or instead to protect as many people as we can.

Chapter 28

FORGING A SUSTAINABLE CLIMATE POLICY

It's time to move beyond the false premise that climate policy necessarily means sacrifices by the present generation.

An effective climate policy for the United States must be sustainable politically as well as environmentally. The environmental requirement – to limit emissions of carbon dioxide and other greenhouse gases so as to prevent massive destabilization of the Earth's climate – is often translated into the policy target of cutting emissions by at least 80 per cent against their 1990 level by the year 2050. Finding a comparable formula for political sustainability has proven more elusive.

Establishing an effective policy is not just a matter of crafting a bill that can pass Congress. The policy must also win public support wide and deep enough to enable it to endure over the decades needed to complete America's transition to a clean energy economy. In other words, the policy must secure support among voters of all partisan persuasions, comparable to that enjoyed by Social Security and Medicare.

To achieve this goal, we must move beyond past strategies that have tried – and failed – to forge a winning political coalition for the clean energy transition. These strategies started from a flawed but widely accepted premise: the assumption that effective climate policy necessarily requires the present generation to make economic sacrifices in order to safeguard the climate for future generations. This framing of the problem has been echoed by environmentalists and fossil fuel firms alike. By ignoring possibilities to design clean energy policies that can benefit the present generation at home – and not only future generations worldwide – this 'eat your broccoli' message fatally undermines political support for effective climate policy.

Benefits Here and Now

Clean energy policy can bring tangible benefits here and now by three avenues:

* *Air quality.* Burning fossil fuels releases not only carbon dioxide but also hazardous air pollutants that harm the health and economic well-being of all Americans, and particularly children whose developing bodies and minds are most susceptible to their toxic impacts. The clean energy transition would prevent thousands of premature deaths, thousands of asthma attacks in children requiring emergency room visits, and millions of lost work days every year.[1] By designing policies that target emissions from sources that impact disadvantaged communities who bear disproportionate pollution burdens, we can protect public health and advance the goal of environmental justice.
* *Employment.* Investments in energy efficiency and clean energy infrastructure will create millions of new jobs for Americans. The job gains come about for two reasons: first, these technologies are more labour-intensive than fossil fuels; and second, the US domestic share of their labour content is higher. Investment in energy efficiency and clean renewables generates more than twice as many jobs per dollar than investment in fossil fuels.[2]
* *Family income.* Last but not least, climate policy can put more money directly into the pockets of the majority of households, protecting the real incomes of middle-class and low-income families even in the face of rising fossil fuel prices. This can be done if, and only if, most or all of the revenue from carbon pricing is returned to the public in the form of equal dividends to every woman, man and child.

Air quality and employment benefits are intrinsic in any effective climate policy, though they can be enhanced by attention paying attention to them when designing specific features of the policy. Whether the third set of benefits – to family incomes – will materialize depends on whether the policy features carbon dividends. Together, these here-and-now benefits can lay the foundation for a climate policy that is sustainable in political as well as environmental terms.

The Politics of Carbon Pricing

A crucial element of climate policy is to put a price on fossil carbon via a fee or cap-and-permit system, so as to limit demand and provide incentives for energy efficiency and alternative energy investments. Carbon pricing poses a great political challenge, however: how to sustain public support for a policy that significantly increases fossil fuel prices, including the most visible price in America – the price of gasoline that is advertised in foot-high numbers on street corners across the land.

The good news is that there is a policy design that can meet this challenge – one that returns the money generated by carbon pricing to the people as dividends (or what economists call 'lump sum payments'). Dividend payments would be highly visible and would ensure that a substantial majority of Americans benefit from climate policy in sheer pocketbook terms: what they receive in dividends would exceed what they pay in higher prices. In my view, this is essential to build durable public support for the climate policy.[3]

The bad news is that these advantages come with an opportunity-cost flip side: every dollar returned to the people as dividends means one less dollar available for the pet priorities of special interests. Legislators and lobbyists of all stripes may not agree on much, but one thing on which they do agree is that they have better uses for money than simply handing it over to the people. Of course, they disagree sharply on exactly what these 'better uses' would be. Environmentalists want to use the money for clean energy and other environmental objectives. Liberals want to use it for social programmes and targeted assistance to those who are most in need. Conservatives want to use it to cut the national debt. Energy corporations want to divert it into windfall profits via a cap-and-giveaway (aka cap-and-trade) policy that gives them free permits. Many economists want to use it to cut 'distortionary' taxes on the grounds that this will create a bigger economic pie.

As each champions their own special interests, none champions dividends. Meanwhile advocates for the public interest in a durable climate policy that brings economic benefits to the majority of Americans have been, with a few laudable exceptions, missing in action. Because no lobbyists represent the people, we must represent ourselves. This turns out to be a tall order.

Carbon Rent

During the 2009 debate on the Waxman-Markey bill, Republican opponents denounced its cap-and-trade plan as a massive hidden tax on American families. Democratic proponents countered that it wasn't really a tax and that the resulting price impacts would be so small – 'less than a postage stamp a day' – that they really wouldn't hurt. The latter claim rested on either confusion or disingenuity. The cost of *preventing* emissions – for example, by insulating buildings or switching to clean energy – may indeed prove to be modest, at least during the early stages of phasing out fossil fuels. But carbon pricing means paying for emissions that are *not* prevented, too, and this can be a much bigger deal.

Resources used to prevent carbon emissions, by installing solar panels or buying more energy-efficient appliances, for example, are not available for other uses. The money that consumers pay in higher fossil fuel prices, in contrast, is not spent on resources but simply transferred. It is *carbon rent*: payment for use of the limited carbon absorptive capacity of the biosphere.

Who will pay carbon rent is a matter of fairly simple economics. Even if the price is levied on firms that bring fossil fuel into the economy – an upstream system that minimizes administrative cost – it will be passed on to consumers. This is desirable as well as inevitable, since the resulting price signals guide consumption and investment decisions. Because upper-income households generally consume more than middle- and lower-income households, they will pay more. But because fuels are a necessity rather than a luxury, middle- and lower-income households will pay more as a *percentage* of their incomes. Carbon pricing itself is therefore regressive, hitting the poor harder than the rich.

Who will receive carbon rent depends on the policy design. Underlying this question is the deeper question of who owns the carbon absorptive capacity of the biosphere. The fossil fuel corporations? The government? Or the people?

Alternative Uses of Carbon Rent

I have already alluded to three reasons why dividends are preferable to other uses of carbon rent. First and foremost, dividends alone can ensure durable public support for climate policy in the face of rising fossil fuel prices. Second, proponents of other uses cannot agree on the best alternative. Third, whatever the merits of other uses, carbon pricing is a regressive way to fund them.

In addition, the merits of many other uses are questionable.

Environmental expenditures: At first blush it may seem that devoting carbon rent to expenditures to wean the economy from fossil fuels would speed the clean energy transition. But as long as the policy puts a hard cap on the use of fossil fuel, such spending would have no effect on total emissions. If we use the money to subsidize the purchase of more efficient electrical appliances, for example, this relieves pressure on the cap and creates more space for emissions from other sources, such as transportation fuels. In other words, earmarking carbon rent for carbon reductions is redundant. Using the money for other environmental purposes not covered by the cap would avoid redundancy but leaves open the possibility of fungibility insofar as that spending otherwise would have been funded from other sources.

Means-tested payments to households: Some liberals advocate returning carbon rent only to households who need it. The Waxman-Markey bill, for example, proposed to allocate 15 per cent of the carbon rent to low-income households. While such a provision would mitigate the regressive impact of carbon pricing, it would raise administrative costs by imposing eligibility tests and raise political costs by excluding the middle class. If, instead of universal coverage, Social Security and Medicare were restricted to low-income households, it is not evident that they would still exist.

Reducing debt: Some conservatives advocate using carbon revenue to pay down the federal government's debt. This is premised on the belief that the US debt/GDP ratio is so high that it weakens the economy. Although the ratio has risen over the past decade, propelled by massive expenditures for the wars in Iraq and Afghanistan, it remains far below the level of the 1940s, when rather than weakening the economy, the debt-financed government spending stimulated it. This does not mean that the sky is the limit for government debt, only that we are nowhere near the sky.

Windfall profits: The political rationale for free permit giveaways to fossil fuel corporations is that letting them capture the carbon rent as windfall profits will neutralize their opposition to climate policy. How well this works can be gauged from the serial failures of cap-and-giveaway proposals in Washington. Moreover, some of the windfall profits would leave the country by going to foreign firms and shareholders. And giveaways require permits to be tradable, creating scope for speculation and trading profits that would drive a further wedge between the carbon rent paid by consumers and the amount available for other uses.

Cutting 'distortionary' taxes: Some economists call for using carbon rent to cut personal and/or corporate income taxes on the grounds that this will grow the economy. Apart from the fact that this would replace progressive taxes with regressive ones, the ostensible economic payoff rests on shaky grounds since it is premised on the assumption that by reducing incentives to supply labour and capital, income taxes today reduce GDP. This would make sense in a theoretical economy where labour and capital are fully employed – if we accept the proposition that Americans really would be better off working longer hours – but in a real-world economy, characterized by chronic unemployment (a.k.a. excess supply of labour) and capital underutilization, it doesn't.

Keeping Government Whole

There is one alternative use for carbon rent for which a good case can be made, though oddly enough, few have made it: keeping the government whole. About 15 per cent of the nation's total carbon footprint is accounted for by local, state and federal government. As in the case of households, a reasonable case can be made for using part of the carbon rent to protect the purchasing power of governments while retaining the price incentives for them to curtail their use of fossil fuels.

To be sure, small government advocates might view the reduction in real government expenditure by carbon pricing as a desirable outcome. The Van Hollen bill, which would distribute 100 per cent of the carbon rent to individuals as non-taxable dividends, would have this effect (see chapter 24). Politically, taxing governments and returning the money to the people could be a selling point for Republicans. But as far as I can tell, they haven't noticed.

There are two ways to tap carbon rent to keep government whole (see chapter 25). One is to take a slice off the top, allocating 25 per cent to government and 75 per cent to dividends, as was proposed in the 2009 Cantwell-Collins bill. The other is to make the dividends to individuals taxable. The two would generate similar amounts of revenue. An attraction of taxable dividends is that much of the revenue would come from progressive income taxation rather than regressive carbon taxation. A potential attraction of the off-the-top option is that the revenue could be earmarked for certain purposes (the list of eligible uses specified in the Cantwell-Collins bill, for example, included transitional adjustment assistance for workers and communities, and international climate mitigation and adaptation assistance).

In either case, mechanisms would need to be established to share the revenue among local, state and federal governments in rough proportion to their carbon footprints. In designing these, a case can be made for allocating more revenue to states with more carbon-intensive electricity sectors as well as more people. Retaining 25 per cent of the carbon rent for governments would create opportunities to channel funds to local school boards, community benefit funds and a 'worker Superfund' to support a just transition for those now employed in the fossil fuel sector – uses that could broaden the policy's appeal to important constituencies.

Dividends and Democracy

Back in 2009 I participated in a conference call of climate policy advocates who were weighing whether to fall into line behind the Waxman-Markey 'cap and trade' bill or instead support the Cantwell-Collins bill with auctioned permits, no permit trading, and carbon dividends. The Waxman-Markey proponents on the call insisted that without giveaways to the corporations, no bill could win backing from the fossil fuel lobby. 'What about backing from the American people?' I asked. They patiently explained that in Washington it's lobbyists who command votes, not voters. My response was, 'Let us assume a democracy.' This provoked much laughter.

Climate policy advocates appear to face a no-win tradeoff when it comes to carbon rent: pander to special interests to win passage in the short term or return the money to the public as dividends to secure durability of the policy in the long term. The first choice is a recipe for long-term failure, while the second seems to be a recipe for short-term failure.

The only exit from this box, in my view, is to mobilize the American people for a carbon price-and-dividend policy. Unless and until the public demands it, we will never get it. And unless we get it, we will not have a politically sustainable climate policy. The picture is as simple – and as complicated – as that.

We cannot assume a democracy. Nor is democracy secured simply by the words written in our Constitution. For democratic rights to be real, they must be exercised. This is hard work. But if forging an effective, sustainable climate policy requires the renewal of American democracy, maybe that's not a bad thing.

NOTES

Chapter 1 Limits to Growth – of What?

1 Adam Liptak, '1 in 100 US Adults behind Bars, New Study Says'. *New York Times*, 28 February 2008.
2 Donella H. Meadows et al., *The Limits to Growth: A Report to the Club of Rome*. New York: Universe Books, 1972.
3 Joseph E. Stiglitz, Amartya Sen and Jean-Paul Fitoussi, *Mismeasuring Our Lives: Why GDP Doesn't Add Up*. New York: New Press, 2010.

Chapter 3 Pursuing Profits – or Power?

1 Lewis F. Powell Jr., 'Confidential Memorandum: Attack on American Free Enterprise System'. 23 August 1971.
2 John Kenneth Galbraith, 'Power and the Useful Economist'. *American Economic Review* 63(1), 1973.
3 William A. Niskanen, 'The Peculiar Economics of Bureaucracy'. *American Economic Review* 58(2), 1968.

Chapter 4 Rent in a Warming World

1 Joseph Stiglitz, *The Price of Inequality*. New York: Norton, 2012.
2 Bill McKibben, 'Global Warming's Terrifying New Math: Three Simple Numbers That Add Up to Global Catastrophe – and That Make Clear Who the Real Enemy Is'. *Rolling Stone*, 19 July 2012. In a 2014 report, *Energy Darwinism II*, Citigroup puts the prospective value of stranded carbon assets higher at $100 trillion.
3 Peter Barnes, 'Cap and Dividend, Not Trade: Making Polluters Pay'. *Scientific American*, December 2008.
4 John M. Broder, 'Cap and Trade Loses Its Standing as Energy Policy of Choice'. *New York Times*, 25 March 2010.

Chapter 5 Universal Assets for Universal Income

1 On the liberal side, see Robert Reich, 'Why We'll Need a Universal Basic Income'. 29 September 2016. Accessed on 14 April 2018 at http://robertreich.org/post/151111696805. On the conservative side, see Noah Gordon, 'The Conservative Case for a Guaranteed Basic Income'. *The Atlantic*, 6 August 2014.

2 Nina Burleigh, 'Sweet U.S. Government Land Deals Charge Up Energy Companies'. *Newsweek*, 27 September 2015.
3 George Packer, 'Obama and Luck'. *New Yorker*, 31 October 2008.
4 'Famous Quotes & Sayings'. Accessed on 14 April 2018 at https://www.quotes.net/quote/55980.
5 Herbert Simon, 'Public Administration in Today's World of Organizations and Markets'. Accessed on 3 February 2018 at https://inst.eecs.berkeley.edu/~cs195/fa14/assets/pdfs/simon_last_lecture.pdf.
6 Robert Pollin and James Heintz, 'Transaction Costs, Trading Elasticities and the Revenue Potential of Financial Transaction Taxes for the United States'. Amherst, MA: Political Economy Research Institute, Research Brief, December 2011. Accessed on 14 April 2018 at http://www.peri.umass.edu/fileadmin/pdf/research_brief/PERI_FTT_Research_Brief.pdf.
7 Robert Frank, 'The Incalculable Value of Finding a Job You Love'. *New York Times*, 22 July 2016.

Chapter 6 Universal Basic Income: Six Questions

1 C. B. Frey and M. A. Osborne, 'The Future of Employment: How Susceptible Are Jobs to Computerization?' *Technological Forecasting and Social Change* 114, January 2017.

Chapter 7 Environmentalism's Original Sin

1 Greg Butcher, 'Common Birds in Decline: A State of the Birds Report'. *Audubon*, Summer 2007. Accessed on 16 April 2018 at http://www.audubon.org/sites/default/files/documents/sotb_cbid_magazine.pdf.
2 Felicity Barringer, 'Meadow Birds in Precipitous Decline, Audubon Says'. *New York Times*, 15 June 2007.
3 Verlyn Klinkenborg, 'Millions of Missing Birds, Vanishing in Plain Sight'. *New York Times*, 19 June 2007.
4 'In Birdsong, a Call to Protect the Earth'. *New York Times*, 22 June 2007.
5 G. S. Butcher and D. K. Niven, 'Combining Data from the Christmas Bird Count and the Breeding Bird Survey to Determine the Continental Status and Trends of North America Birds'. Ivyland, PA: National Audubon Society, June 2007. Accessed on 18 April 2018 at http://web4.audubon.org/bird/stateofthebirds/cbid/content/Report.pdf.
6 James P. Robson and Fikret Berkes, 'Exploring Some of the Myths of Land Use Change: Can Rural to Urban Migration Drive Declines in Biodiversity?' *Global Environmental Change* 21(3), August 2011.
7 Wallace Stegner, *Beyond the Hundredth Meridian: John Wesley Powell and the Opening of the West*. Boston: Houghton Mifflin, 1954.
8 William Cronon, 'The Trouble with Wilderness; or, Getting Back to the Wrong Nature'. In William Cronon, ed., *Uncommon Ground: Rethinking the Human Place in Nature*, New York: W.W. Norton, 1995.

Chapter 8 Rethinking Extinction

1 Quoted in Joel Greenberg, *A Feathered River Across the Sky: The Passenger Pigeon's Flight to Extinction*. New York: Bloomsbury, 2014, p. 187.

2 Quoted in A.W. Schorger, *The Passenger Pigeon: Its Natural History and Extinction*. Madison: University of Wisconsin Press, 1955, p. 61.

3 Mark Cocker, *Birds & People*. London: Random House, 2013, p. 241.

4 Quoted in Greenberg, p. 54.

5 Quoted in Mark V. Barrow, *Nature's Ghosts: Confronting Extinction from the Age of Jefferson to the Age of Ecology*. Chicago: University of Chicago Press, 2009, p. 15.

6 Elizabeth Kolbert, *The Sixth Extinction: An Unnatural History*. New York: Henry Holt, 2014, p. 54.

7 Thomas DeVoe, *The Market Assistant*. New York: Hurd & Houghton, 1867.

8 Schorger, p. 130.

9 Ibid., p. 186.

10 Greenberg, p. 142.

11 Ibid., p. 210.

12 Greenberg, p. 211.

13 Schorger, p. 223.

14 Quoted in Nathaniel Rich, 'The Mammoth Cometh'. *New York Times Magazine*, 27 February 2014.

15 Ibid.

16 David Blockstein, lecture at the University of Rhode Island, 27 February 2014.

17 Quoted by Cocker, p. 461.

Chapter 9 Inequality and the Environment

1 Betsy Hartmann and James K. Boyce, *A Quiet Violence: View from a Bangladesh Village*. London: Zed Press, 1983.

2 Amartya Sen, *Poverty and Famines*. Oxford: Oxford University Press, 1981.

3 James K. Boyce, *Agrarian Impasse in Bengal: Institutional Constraints to Technological Change*. Oxford and New York: Oxford University Press, 1987.

4 Mariano Torras and James K. Boyce, 'Income, Inequality, and Pollution: A Reassessment of the Environmental Kuznets Curve'. *Ecological Economics* 25, 1998; reprinted in James K. Boyce, *The Political Economy of the Environment*. Cheltenham, U.K., and Northampton, MA: Edward Elgar, 2002.

5 James K. Boyce et al., 'Power Distribution, the Environment, and Public Health: A State-Level Analysis'. *Ecological Economics*, 29, 1999; reprinted in James K. Boyce, *The Political Economy of the Environment*. Cheltenham, U.K., and Northampton, MA: Edward Elgar, 2002.

6 Bina Agarwal, *Gender and Green Governance: The Political Economy of Women's Presence Within and Beyond Community Forestry*. Oxford: Oxford University Press, 2010.

7 For more on the impacts of inequality on the environment, see: T. G. Holland, G. D. Peterson and A. Gonzalez, 'A Cross-National Analysis of How Economic Inequality Predicts Biodiversity Loss'. *Conservation Biology* 23(5), 2010; J. Baek and G. Gweisah, 'Does Income Inequality Harm the Environment? Empirical Evidence from the United States'. *Energy Policy* 62, 2013; L. Cushing, R. Morello-Frosch, M. Wander and M. Pastor, 'The Haves, the Have-Nots, and the Health of Everyone: The Relationship Between Social Inequality and Environmental Quality'. *Annual Review of Public Health* 36, 2014; and J.K. Boyce, 'The Environmental Cost of Inequality,' *Scientific American*, November 2018.

8 Robert D. Bullard, 'Solid Waste Sites and the Black Houston Community'. *Sociological Inquiry* 53, 1983.

9 See, for example: M. Ash and T. R. Fetter, 'Who Lives on the Wrong Side of the Environmental Tracks?' *Social Science Quarterly* 85(2), 2004; R. D. Bullard, 'Equity, Unnatural Man-Made Disasters, and Race'. In R. C. Wilkinson and W. R. Freudenburg, eds., *Equity and the Environment (Research in Social Problems and Public Policy, Volume 15)*. Bingley, U.K.: Emerald Group Publishing, 2008; and P. Mohai and R. Saha, 'Which Came First, People or Pollution? A Review of Theory and Evidence from Longitudinal Environmental Justice Studies'. *Environmental Research Letters* 10(12), 2015.

10 James K. Boyce, Klara Zwickl and Michael Ash, 'Measuring Environmental Inequality'. *Ecological Economics* 124, 2016.

11 Manuel Pastor, James Sadd and Rachel Morello-Frosch, 'Who's Minding the Kids? Toxic Air, Public Schools, and Environmental Justice in Los Angeles'. *Social Science Quarterly* 83(1), 2002. See also: Janet Currie et al., 'Does Pollution Increase School Absences?' *Review of Economics and Statistics* 91(4), 2009; Cristina Lucier et al., 'Toxic Pollution and School Performance Scores: Environmental Ascription in East Baton Rouge Parish, Louisiana'. *Organization & Environment*, 24(4), 2011; and Paul Mohai et al., 'Air Pollution around Schools Is Linked to Poorer Student Health and Academic Performance'. *Health Affairs* 30(5), 2011.

12 See, for example: Kenneth Chay and Michael Greenstone, 'The Impact of Air Pollution on Infant Mortality: Evidence from Geographic Variation in Pollution Shocks Induced by a Recession'. *Quarterly Journal of Economics* 118(3), 2003; Janet Currie and Matthew Neidell, 'Air Pollution and Infant Health: What Can We Learn from California's Recent Experience?' *Quarterly Journal of Economics* 120(3), 2005; and Janet Currie et al., 'Air Pollution and Infant Health: Lessons from New Jersey'. *Journal of Health Economics* 28, 2009.

13 On property values, see Janet Currie et al., 'Environmental Health Risks and Housing Values: Evidence from 1,600 Toxic Plant Openings and Closings'. *American Economic Review* 105(2), 2015. On work-day losses, see Neal Fann et al., 'The Recent and Future Health Burden of Air Pollution Apportioned Across U.S. Sectors'. *Environmental Science & Technology* 47(8), 2013. On health care costs, see U.S. Environmental Protection Agency, 'Mercury and Air Toxics Standards: Healthier Americans'. Washington, DC: USEPA, 2014.

14 'Two in Three Call Climate Change Serious; Many Still See Scientific Disagreement'. ABC News/Washington Post poll, 30 November 2015. Accessed on 2 April 2018 at http://www.langerresearch.com/wp-content/uploads/1173a5ClimateChange.pdf.

15 Michael Ash et al., 'Is Environmental Justice Good for White Folks? Industrial Air Toxics Exposure in Urban America'. *Social Science Quarterly* 94(3), 2012. See chapter 10.

16 For more from the Natural Assets Project, see James K. Boyce and Barry G. Shelley, eds. *Natural Assets: Democratizing Environmental Ownership*. Washington, DC: Island Press, 2003; and James K. Boyce, Sunita Narain and Elizabeth A. Stanton, eds. *Reclaiming Nature: Environmental Justice and Ecological Restoration*. London: Anthem Press, 2007.

17 For more on crop genetic diversity and its conservation by small farmers, see: Stephen B. Brush, *Farmers' Bounty: Locating Crop Diversity in the Contemporary World*. New Haven, CT: Yale University Press, 2004; Charles C. Mann, *Diversity on the Farm*. New York: Ford Foundation (https://www.peri.umass.edu/fileadmin/pdf/Mann.pdf); and James K. Boyce, 'A Future for Small Farms? Biodiversity and Sustainable Agriculture'. in J. K. Boyce et al., eds., *Human Development in the Era of Globalization: Essays in Honor of Keith B. Griffin*. Northampton, MA: Edward Elgar, 2006 (reprinted in J. K. Boyce,

Economics, the Environment and Our Common Wealth. Cheltenham, U.K., and Northampton, MA: Edward Elgar, 2013).

18 Manuel Pastor et al., *In the Wake of the Storm: Environment, Disaster, and Race After Katrina.* New York: Russell Sage Foundation, 2006.

19 James K. Boyce and Manuel Pastor, 'Clearing the Air: Incorporating Air Quality and Environmental Justice into Climate Policy'. *Climatic Change* 102(4), 2013; James K. Boyce, 'Distributional Issues in Climate Policy: Air Quality Co-benefits and Carbon Rent'. Forthcoming in Graciela Chichilnisky and Armon Rezai, eds., *Handbook on the Economics of Climate Change.* Cheltenham and Northampton: Edward Elgar Press, 2019.

20 Robert Pollin et al., *Green Growth: A U.S. Program for Controlling Climate Change and Expanding Job Opportunities.* Amherst, MA: Political Economy Research Institute and Washington, DC: Center for American Progress, 2014; Robert Pollin, *Greening the Global Economy.* Cambridge, MA: MIT Press, 2015.

21 This is not to say that carbon pricing ought to entirely supplant other elements in the climate policy toolkit, such as regulation and public investment. A smart policy mix would use more than one instrument (see chapter 17). For example, smart regulations can complement a carbon price by promoting research and development of new technologies or by ensuring emission reductions from sources with the greatest air quality co-benefits. Public investments, ranging from local projects to retrofit school buildings to national projects to rebuild rail transport infrastructure, are clearly important parts of the mix, too. One can accept that carbon pricing is necessary without claiming that it is sufficient.

22 While this is true in industrialized economies, the picture may be different in low-income countries. Data from China in 1995, for example, indicate that carbon pricing at the time would have been progressive: upper-income households spent more on fossil fuels not only absolutely but also as a percentage of their expenditure (Mark Brenner et al., 'A Chinese Sky Trust? Distributional Impacts of Carbon Charges and Revenue Recycling in China'. *Energy Policy* 35, 2007).

23 James K. Boyce and Matthew Riddle, *CLEAR Economics: State-Level Impacts of the Carbon Limits and Energy for America's Renewal Act.* Amherst, MA: Political Economy Research Institute, 2011; James K. Boyce, 'The Carbon Dividend'. *New York Times,* 30 July 2014.

24 Peter Barnes, *With Liberty and Dividends for All: How to Save Our Middle Class When Jobs Don't Pay Enough.* San Francisco: Berrett-Koehler, 2014. See also chapter 5.

Chapter 10 Clean Air for All

1 See, for example, R. Morello-Frosch et al., 'Understanding the cumulative impacts of inequalities in environmental health: implications for policy'. *Health Affairs* 30(5), May 2011.

2 Michael Ash et al., 'Is Environmental Justice Good for White Folks? Industrial Air Toxics Exposure in Urban America'. *Social Science Quarterly* 94(3), June 2012.

Chapter 11 Letter from Flint

1 The role of the Women's Emergency Brigade is told in the 1979 Academy Award-nominated documentary film *With Babies and Banners.*

2 Audio recordings of strikers are archived at Michigan State University's 'The Flint Sit-Down Strike: Audio Gallery'. Accessed on 23 April 2018 at http://flint.matrix.msu.edu/strike.php.
3 Ceci Connolly, 'U.S. Firms Losing Health Care Battle, GM Chairman Says'. *Washington Post*, 11 February 2005.

Chapter 12 Let them Drink Pollution?

1 'Let Them Eat Pollution'. *Economist*, 8 February 1992.
2 'Statement by Douglas M. Costle on Enactment of the Clean Water Act of 1977'. EPA Press Release, 28 December 1977. Accessed on 24 April 2018 at http://www.agriculturedefensecoalition.org/sites/default/files/pdfs/4P_1977_EPA_Press_Release_December_28_1977_President_Carter_Clear_Water_Act_Clean_Air_Act_Amendments_in_1977.pdf.
3 U.S. Environmental Protection Agency, 'Mortality Risk Valuation'. Accessed on 24 April 2018 at https://www.epa.gov/environmental-economics/mortality-risk-valuation. The official VSL is $7.4 million in 2006 dollars; $9.1 million is its inflation-adjusted value in 2018.
4 See the discussion of the power-weighted social decision rule in chapter 9.
5 Jiquanda Johnson, 'Flint, Detroit among Nation's Poorest Cities, New Census Data Show'. *mLive.com*, 17 September 2015. Accessed on 24 April 2018 at http://www.mlive.com/news/flint/index.ssf/2015/09/flint_detroit_among_nations_po.html; Christopher Ingram, 'This Is How Toxic Flint's Water Really Is'. *Washington Post*, 15 January 2016.
6 Stephen Rodrick, 'Who Poisoned Flint, Michigan?' *Rolling Stone*, 22 January 2016.
7 Abby Goodnough, Monica Davey and Mitch Smith, 'When the Water Turned Brown'. *New York Times*, 23 January 2016.
8 Mona Hanna-Attisha et al., 'Elevated Blood Lead Levels in Children Associated with the Flint Drinking Water Crisis'. *American Journal of Public Health* 106(2), February 2016; Julie Bosman, Monica Davey and Mitch Smith, 'As Water Problems Grew, Officials Belittled Complaints From Flint'. *New York Times*, 20 January 2016.
9 Scott Bixby, 'Michigan Governor Says Environmental Racism Not to Blame for Flint Crisis'. *The Guardian*, 22 January 2016.
10 'Depraved Indifference Toward Flint'. *New York Times*, 22 January 2016.
11 Steve Lerner, *Sacrifice Zones: The Front Lines of Toxic Chemical Exposure in the United States*. Cambridge, MA: MIT Press, 2010.

Chapter 13 Letter from Delhi

1 Sarath K. Guttikunda and Giuseppe Calori, 'A GIS Based Emissions Inventory at 1 km × 1 km Spatial Resolution for Air Pollution Analysis in Delhi, India'. *Atmospheric Environment* 67, March 2013.
2 'Delhi's Residents Are Breathing Worse Air than Previously Known'. *The Hindu*, 12 December 2014.
3 Ami Sedghi, 'Air Pollution: Delhi Is Dirty, but How Do Other Cities Fare?' *The Guardian*, 24 June 2015.
4 Chetan Chauhan, 'Beijing Better than Delhi: Only 7 Days of Good Air in Capital in 2yrs'. *Hindustan Times*, 22 April 2015.

5 'U.S. to Transport 20,000 Gallons of Breathable Air for Obama's Visit to Delhi for Republic Day'. *Unreal Times*, 18 January 2015. Accessed on 24 April 2018 at http://www.theunrealtimes.com/2015/01/18/us-to-transport-20000-gallons-of-breathable-air-for-obamas-visit-to-delhi-for-republic-day/.

6 Natalie Obiko Pearson, 'Mr. President, World's Worst Air Is Taking 6 Hours Off Your Life'. *Bloomberg.com*, 26 January 2015. Accessed on 24 April 2018 at https://www.bloomberg.com/news/articles/2015-01-26/mr-president-world-s-worst-air-is-taking-6-hours-off-your-life.

7 Andrew Foster and Naresh Kumar, 'Health Effects of Air Quality Regulations in Delhi, India'. *Atmospheric Environment* 45, 2011.

8 Amit Garg, 'Pro-equity Effects of Ancillary Benefits of Climate Change Policies: A Case Study of Human Health Impacts of Outdoor Air Pollution in New Delhi'. *World Development* 39(6), 2011.

9 Central Pollution Control Board, 'Study on Ambient Air Quality, Respiratory Symptoms and Lung Function of Children in Delhi'. New Delhi: Ministry of Environment & Forests, September 2008.

10 Quoted in Aniruddha Ghosal and Pritha Chaterjee, 'Landmark Study Lies Buried: How Delhi's Poisonous Air Is Damaging its Children for Life'. *Indian Express*, 2 April 2015.

11 Joshua S. Apte et al., 'Concentrations of Fine, Uultrafine, and Black Carbon Particles in Auto-Rickshaws in New Delhi, India'. *Atmospheric Environment* 45, August 2011.

12 Edward Wong, 'China Blocks Web Access to "Under the Dome" Documentary on Pollution'. *New York Times*, 6 March 2015. Elsewhere the film can be accessed (with English subtitles) at https://www.youtube.com/watch?v=T6X2uwlQGQM&feature=youtu.be.

13 Accessed on 24 April 2018 at http://indianexpress.com/about/death-by-breath/.

14 Gardiner Harris, 'Delhi Wakes Up to an Air Pollution Problem It Cannot Ignore'. *New York Times*, 14 February 2015.

15 Gardiner Harris, 'Holding Your Breath in India'. *New York Times*, 29 May 2015.

16 'Want to Make Delhi a World-Class City Like Barcelona, Policies to Follow Soon'. *Indian Express*, 4 January 2015..

17 Aseem Shrivastava and James K. Boyce, 'Green goals for the Delhi *Aam Aadmi*'. *The Hindu*, 1 May 2015.

Chapter 14 Mapping the Environmental Riskscape

1 For overviews, see Eric J. Ringquist, 'Assessing Evidence of Environmental Inequities: A Meta-Analysis'. *Journal of Policy Analysis and Management* 24(2), 2005; and Paul Mohai and Robin Saha, 'Reassessing Racial and Socioeconomic Disparities in Environmental Justice Research'. *Demography* 43(2), 2006.

2 Klara Zwickl, Michael Ash and James K. Boyce, 'Regional Variation in Environmental Inequality: Industrial Air Toxics exposure in U.S. cities'. *Ecological Economics* 107, 2014.

3 Ibid., Table 1.

Chapter 15 Measuring Pollution Inequality

1 James K. Boyce, Klara Zwickl and Michael Ash, 'Three Measures of Environmental Inequality'. Institute for New Economic Thinking (INET), Working Group on the Political Economy of Distribution, Working Paper No. 4. May 2015. A revised version

of the paper was later published as 'Measuring Environmental Inequality'. *Ecological Economics* 124, 2016.

2 Manuel Pastor, James Sadd and Rachel Morello-Frosch, 'Who's Minding the Kids? Toxic Air, Public Schools, and Environmental Justice in Los Angeles'. *Social Science Quarterly* 83(1), 2002.

3 Ian Parry, Chandara Veung and Dirk Heine, 'How Much Carbon Pricing is in Countries' Own Interests? The Critical Role of Co-Benefits'. Washington, DC: International Monetary Fund, Working Paper WP/14/174, September 2014.

Chapter 16 Cleaning the Air and Cooling the Planet

1 International Institute for Applied Systems Analysis, *Global Energy Assessment: Toward a Sustainable Future*. Cambridge: Cambridge University Press, 2012.

2 M. M. Berk et al., 'Sustainable Energy: Trade-Offs and Synergies between Energy Security, Competitiveness, and Environment'. Bilthoven: Netherlands Environmental Assessment Agency, 2006.

3 See James K. Boyce and Manuel Pastor, 'Cooling the Planet, Clearing the Air: Climate Policy, Carbon Pricing, and Co-Benefits'. Economics for Equity and the Environment Network, September 2012. Online at http://www.peri.umass.edu/fileadmin/pdf/published_study/Cooling_the_Planet_Sept2012-1.pdf.

4 Ibid.

Chapter 17 Smart Climate Policy

1 James Heintz, Robert Pollin and Heidi Garrett-Peltier, *How Infrastructure Investments Support the U.S. Economy: Employment, Productivity and Growth*. Amherst, MA: Political Economy Research Institute, January 2009. Online at http://www.peri.umass.edu/fileadmin/pdf/other_publication_types/green_economics/PERI_Infrastructure_Investments.

2 Quoted in 'Obama's Cap-and-Trade Plan Faces a Fight in Congress (Update 1)'. *Bloomberg.com*, 8 December 2008.

3 McKinsey & Co., 'Reducing U.S. Greenhouse Gas Emissions: How Much at What Cost?' December 2007. Accessed on 25 April 2018 at https://www.mckinsey.com/business-functions/sustainability-and-resource-productivity/our-insights/reducing-us-greenhouse-gas-emissions.

4 Robert Pollin, 'Financing the Green Economy as an Answer to Casino Capitalism'. *New Labor Forum* 18(1), Winter 2009.

Chapter 18 Investment in Disadvantaged Communities

1 National Academy of Sciences (NAS), *Hidden Costs of Energy: Unpriced Consequences of Energy Production and Use*. Washington, DC: NAS, 2009.

2 CARB, *Climate Change Scoping Plan: A Framework for Change*. Pursuant to AB 32, The California Global Warming Solutions Act of 2006, December 2008, p. 70.

3 CARB, 'Climate Change Scoping Plan, Resolution 08-47'. 11 December 2009, p. 8.

4 Recommendations of the Economic and Technology Advancement Advisory Committee (ETAAC), Final Report. 11 February 2008, p. 2–5.

5 Similarly, the purchase of offsets is constrained or proscribed altogether in high-priority zones. In the presence of co-pollutants, the purchase of offsets from out-of-state has the effect of exporting the co-benefits from air quality improvements. In the same way, offsets would result in the loss of co-benefits from co-pollutant reduction in high-priority zones. See David Roland-Holst, 'Carbon Emission Offsets and Criteria Pollutants: A California Assessment'. Berkeley: University of California Berkeley, Center for Energy, Resources, and Economic Sustainability, Research Paper No. 0903091, March 2009.

6 Lata Gangadharan, 'Analysis of prices in tradable emission markets: An empirical study of the Regional Clean Air Incentives Market in Los Angeles'. *Applied Economics* 36, 2004.

7 Tom Tietenberg, 'Tradeable permits for pollution control when emission location matters: What have we learned?' *Environmental and Resource Economics* 5, 1995.

8 The significance of plant-to-plant variations in co-pollutant intensity is underscored in the National Academy of Sciences study. See the comments of Professor Maureen Cropper, vice-chair of the NAS committee that produced the study, quoted in Matthew Wald, 'Fossil Fuels' Hidden Cost is in Billions, Study Says'. *New York Times,* 20 October 2009.

9 Lisa M. Berry, 'Inequality in the Creation of Environmental Harm: Looking for Answers from Within'. in Robert C. Wilkinson and William R. Freudenberg, eds., *Equity and the Environment: Research in Social Problems and Public Policy, Volume 15.* Amsterdam: Elsevier, 2008.

Chapter 19 Dividends for All

1 Carbon permits themselves are not property rights. Just as buying a parking permit is not the same as owning the parking lot, buying a carbon permit is not the same as owning the property created by a carbon cap. A carbon permit allows the holder to 'park' carbon in the atmosphere. The property may be owned by the government (if permits are auctioned and the revenue is used by the state), by firms (if they receive free permit allocations), or by the people (if permits are auctioned and the revenue is returned to the public).

2 For estimates of the distributional impact of a California-only cap-and-dividend policy, see the memorandum to EAAC from Cathy Kunkel and Daniel M. Kammen dated 2 November 2009, accessed on 28 April 2018 at http://www.climatechange.ca.gov/ eaac/documents/member_materials/Kunkel_and_Kammen_Cap_and_Dividend_ memo.pdf.

3 Robert Greenstein et al., 'Designing Climate-Change Legislation that Shields Low-Income Households from Increased Poverty and Hardship'. Washington, DC: Center for Budget and Policy Priorities, 9 May 2008. Accessed on 28 April 2018 at http:// www.cbpp.org/files/10-25-07climate.pdf.

4 James K. Boyce and Matthew E. Riddle, 'Cap and Dividend: A State-by-State Analysis'. Amherst, MA: Political Economy Research Institute, August 2009, Figure 6.

5 For details on logistics of the Alaska Permanent Fund, see its website at https://pfd. alaska.gov/.

6 For details, see James K. Boyce memorandum to EAAC, 'Electronic Funds Transfer'. 13 December 2009. Accessed on 28 April 2018 at http://www.climatechange.ca.gov/ eaac/documents/member_materials/Boyce%20memo%20on%20Electronic%20 Funds%20Transfer%2012-13-09.pdf.

Chapter 20 Truth Spill

1 Quoted by Jill Leovy, 'BP's Containment Problem is Unprecedented'. *Los Angeles Times*, 30 April 2010.

2 For footage, see https://www.youtube.com/watch?v=XoE82VIjqn4.

3 Justin Gillis, 'Giant Plumes of Oil Forming Under the Gulf'. *New York Times*, 15 May 2010.

4 Elisabeth Rosenthal, 'In Gulf of Mexico, Chemicals Under Scrutiny'. *New York Times*, 5 May 2010.

5 Charlie Savage, 'Sex, Drug Use and Graft Cited in Interior Department'. *New York Times*, 10 September 2008.

6 Cain Burdeau and Holbrook Mohr, 'BP Downplayed Possibility of Major Oil Spill'. *Boston Globe*, 1 May 2010.

7 Katie Couric, 'As Oil Spews in the Gulf, Anger Grows on Shore'. *CBS News*, 24 May 2010. Accessed on 28 April 2018 at https://www.cbsnews.com/news/as-oil-spews-in-the-gulf-anger-grows-on-shore/; Leslie Kaufman, 'Controlled Burn Considered for Gulf Oil Spill'. *New York Times*, 27 April 2010.

8 Matthew L. Wald and Tom Zeller Jr., 'Fishing Ban Is Expanded as Spill Impact Becomes More Evident'. *New York Times*, 18 May 2010.

9 John M. Broder, Campbell Robertson and Clifford Krauss, 'Amount of Spill Could Escalate, Company Admits'. *New York Times*, 4 May 2010.

10 'Fox News: Ocean Can Handle Oil Spill'. 17 May 2010, accessed on 28 April 2018 at https://www.youtube.com/watch?v=PFmBedwbVWU; Russell Goldman, 'Limbaugh, Scientists Square Off on Oil Spill Cleanup'. *ABC News*, 3 May 2010. Accessed on 28 April 2018 at http://abcnews.go.com/Technology/limbaugh-environmentalists-square-off-blame-oil-leak/story?id=10542582.

11 Jad Mouawad, 'The Spill vs. a Need to Drill'. *New York Times*, 1 May 2010.

12 John Kenneth Galbraith, 'Power and the Useful Economist'. *American Economic Review* 63(1), 1973, p. 9.

13 'Uncertainty About Oil Spill Size'. *Fox News*, 30 April 2010. Accessed on 28 April 2018 at http://video.foxnews.com/v/4197219/?playlist_id=86856#sp=show-clips.

14 Ian R. MacDonald et al., 'The Measure of a Disaster'. *New York Times*, 21 May 2010.

15 'The Latest on the Oil Spill'. *New York Times*, 21 May 2010.

16 Lisa Margonelli, 'A Spill of Our Own'. *New York Times*, 1 May 2010.

17 'A West Virginia Coal Mine Explosion Demands Action'. *Washington Post*, 7 April 2010; Ellen Barry, 'Rescuers Are Counted Among Dead as Toll Rises in Russian Mine Blasts'. *New York Times*, 10 May 2010; and Keith Bradsher, 'At Least 92 Die in Chinese Mine Explosion'. *New York Times*, 21 November 2009.

18 Clifford Krauss and Elisabeth Rosenthal, 'Reliance on Oil Sands Grows Despite Environmental Risks'. *New York Times*, 18 May 2010.

19 National Academy of Sciences (NAS), *Hidden Costs of Energy: Unpriced Consequences of Energy Production and Use*. Washington, DC: NAS, 2009.

20 'Another Step Towards Securing Our Future in Energy'. 21 May 2010. Accessed on 28 April 2018 at https://obamawhitehouse.archives.gov/blog/2010/05/21/another-step-towards-securing-our-future-energy.

Chapter 21 Four Pillars of Climate Justice

1 'Let Them Eat Pollution'. *The Economist*, 8 February 1992.
2 James K. Boyce and Manuel Pastor, 'Clearing the Air: Incorporating Air Quality and Environmental Justice into Climate Policy'. *Climatic Change* 102(4), 2013.

Chapter 22 The Perverse Logic of Offsets

1 E. K. Hunt and Ralph d'Arge, 'On Lemmings and Other Acquisitive Animals: Propositions on Consumption'. *Journal of Economic Issues* 7, June 1973, p. 348.
2 Elisabeth Rosenthal and Andrew W. Lehren, 'Profits on Carbon Credits Drive Output of a Harmful Gas'. *New York Times*, 8 August 2012.
3 Elisabeth Rosenthal, 'In a Factory's Shadow, Fears About Health'. *New York Times*, 8 August 2012.
4 Quoted in 'China's Greenhouse Gas Vent Threat in Bid to Export Billions'. Environmental Investigation Agency, 8 November 2011. Accessed on 29 April 2018 at http://eia-international.org/china-threat-to-vent-super-greenhouse-gases-in-bid-to-extort-billions.
5 Quoted in Rosenthal, 'In a Factory's Shadow, Fears About Health'.

Chapter 23 Climate Policy as Wealth Creation

1 Congressional Budget Office, 'An Evaluation of Cap-and-Trade Programs for Reducing U.S. Carbon Emissions'. Washington, DC, June 2001. Accessed on 3 May 2018 at https://www.cbo.gov/sites/default/files/107th-congress-2001-2002/reports/captrade.pdf.
2 'Obama Implores Senate to Pass Climate Bill'. *NBC News*, 27 June 2009. Accessed on 3 May 2018 at http://www.nbcnews.com/id/31565446/ns/us_news-environment/t/obama-implores-senate-pass-climate-bill/.
3 McKinsey & Co., 'Pathways to a Low-Carbon Economy: Version 2 of the Global Greenhouse Gas Abatement Cost Curve'. September 2013. Accessed on 3 May 2018 at https://www.mckinsey.com/business-functions/sustainability-and-resource-productivity/our-insights/pathways-to-a-low-carbon-economy.
4 Julie Bosman, 'Unlikely Allies Campaign for a Gas-Tax Holiday'. *New York Times*, 2 May 2008.

Chapter 24 The Carbon Dividend

1 Van Hollen reintroduced this legislation after being elected to the U.S. Senate in 2016. The bill can be accessed online at https://www.govtrack.us/congress/bills/115/s2352/text.

Chapter 25 Keeping the Government Whole

1 Based on data for the year 2002. This is close to the estimate of 13 per cent for 1998 by Terry Dinan and Diane Rogers, 'Distributional Effects of Carbon Allowance Trading'. *National Tax Journal* 55, 2002, p. 205.

2 Dinan and Rogers, p. 211. These authors also add small impacts imputed to 'deadweight losses' and the tax impact of reduced GDP growth, arriving at total net effects on government equivalent to 29.6 per cent of carbon revenue. Both adjustments are open to question: the welfare losses ignore the welfare gains that are the rationale for a carbon policy in the first place; and there is no consensus as to the magnitude or even the sign of the effects of a carbon policy on GDP growth.

3 For details, see James K. Boyce and Matthew Riddle, 'Keeping the Government Whole'. Amherst, MA: Political Economy Research Institute, Working Paper No. 188, November 2008. The income and sales tax revenues are based solely on the dividends received and spent by households. Our calculations do not include 'multiplier effects' or income tax revenues from firms.

4 Both government and households can come out ahead because there are two additional sources of carbon revenue: non-profit institutions and buyers of US exports. Like households and government, they pay higher prices for fossil fuels (and for everything that is produced and distributed by using them), but they receive no compensation. Our calculations assume that imports are subject to 'carbon tariffs' equivalent to the carbon price embodied in the prices of domestically produced goods and services. If carbon tariffs are not levied on imported goods (or, for administrative simplicity, they are levied only on the high-carbon subset of imported goods), this will correspondingly decrease both the charge to consumers and amount that households receive as dividends, leaving average net benefits unchanged.

Chapter 26 Air Quality Co-benefits in Climate Policy

1 World Health Organization (WHO), '7 Million Premature Deaths Annually Linked to Air Pollution'. Geneva: WHO News Release, 25 March 2014. Accessed on 4 May 2018 at http://www.who.int/mediacentre/news/releases/2014/air-pollution/en/.

2 OECD, *The Cost of Air Pollution: Health Impacts of Road Transport*. Paris, 2014, pp. 53–55.

3 Cass Sunstein, *Valuing Life: Humanizing the Regulatory State*. Chicago: University of Chicago Press, 2014, p. 89.

4 Ibid., p. 90.

5 J. Lelieveld et al., 'The Contribution of Outdoor Air Pollution Sources to Premature Mortality on a Global Scale'. *Nature* 525, 2015.

6 The official VSL used by the US Environmental Protection Agency (EPA) in 2013 was $9.7 million. For discussion, see EPA, 'Valuing Mortality Risk Reductions for Policy: A Meta-analytic Approach' prepared by the US Environmental Protection Agency's Office of Policy, National Center for Environmental Economics, for review by the EPA's Science Advisory Board, Environmental Economics Advisory Committee. February 2016, p. 2. Accessed on 6 May 2018 at https://yosemite.epa.gov/sab/sabproduct.nsf/0/0CA9E925C9A702F285257F380050C842/$File/VSL%20white%20paper_final_020516.pdf.

7 EPA, 'EPA Fact Sheet: Social Cost of Carbon'. December 2016. Accessed on 6 May 2018 at https://www.epa.gov/sites/production/files/2016-12/documents/social_cost_of_carbon_fact_sheet.pdf. For critiques of the methods used to calculate the SCC, see Frank Ackerman and Elizabeth A. Stanton, 'Climate Risks and Carbon prices: Revising the Social Cost of Carbon'. *Economics: The Open-Access, Open-Assessment E-Journal* 6, 2012, and Robert S. Pindyck, 'Climate Change Policy: What Do the Models Tell Us?' *Journal of Economic Literature* 51(3), 2013.

8 Chris Mooney, 'New EPA Document Reveals Sharply Lower Estimate of the Cost of Climate Change'. *Washington Post*, 11 October 2017.

9 Drew T. Shindell et al., 'Climate and Health Impacts of US Emissions Reductions Consistent with 2°C'. *Nature Climate Change*, 2016.

10 M. Berk et al., 'Sustainable Energy: Trade-Offs and Synergies between Energy Security, Competitiveness, and Environment'. Technical report, Bilthoven: Netherlands Environmental Assessment Agency, 2006.

11 Manuel Pastor et al., 'Risky Business: Cap-and-Trade, Public Health, and Environmental Justice'. In C. G. Boone and M. Fragkias, eds., *Urbanization and Sustainability*. Dordrecht: Springer Netherlands, 2013.

12 S. Bonorris, ed., *Environmental Justice for All: A Fifty State Survey of Legislation, Policies and Cases*, 4th edn. Berkeley: American Bar Association and Hastings College of the Law, University of California, 2010.

13 James K. Boyce and Manuel Pastor, 'Clearing the Air: Incorporating Air Quality and Environmental Justice into Climate Policy'. *Climatic Change*, 120(4), 2013.

14 OMB, 'Circular A-4'. 17 September 2003. Accessed on 6 May 2018 at https://www. transportation.gov/sites/dot.gov/files/docs/OMB%20Circular%20No.%20A-4.pdf.

15 For discussion, see Vien Truong, 'Addressing Poverty and Pollution: California's SB 535 Greenhouse Gas Reduction Fund'. *Harvard Civil Rights-Civil Liberties Law Review* 49(2), 2014.

Chapter 27 Climate Adaptation: Protecting Money or People?

1 'Let Them Eat Pollution'. *Economist*, 8 February 1992.

Chapter 28 Forging a Sustainable Climate Policy

1 Drew T. Shindell et al., 'Climate and Health Impacts of US Emissions Reductions Consistent with 2°C'. *Nature Climate Change*, 2016.

2 Robert Pollin, *Greening the Global Economy*. Cambridge, MA: MIT Press, 2015.

3 For more carbon dividends, see preceding chapters and James K. Boyce, *The Case for Carbon Dividends*. London: Polity Press, 2019.

PUBLICATION HISTORY

Earlier versions of these essays appeared in the following venues:

Chapter 1: *TripleCrisis*, 27 June 2013.
Chapter 2: 'Confronting the Twin Tragedies of Open Access', *UN Dispatch*, 21 September 2007.
Chapter 3: *Dollars & Sense*, July/August 2013.
Chapter 4: *TripleCrisis*, 19 March 2014.
Chapter 5: *TripleCrisis*, 7 November 2016.
Chapter 6: 'Are We Ready for Universal Basic Income?' Interview with *Vita International*, 2 December 2016.
Chapter 7: *TripleCrisis*, 9 August 2011.
Chapter 8: *Harper's Magazine*, November 2015.
Chapter 9: Leontief Prize Lecture, Tufts University, March 2017.
Chapter 10: *TripleCrisis*, 6 December 2012.
Chapter 11: *TripleCrisis*, 31 August 2010.
Chapter 12: *Institute for New Economic Thinking*, 26 January 2016.
Chapter 13: *TripleCrisis*, 20 and 27 July 2015.
Chapter 14: *TripleCrisis*, 25 May 2015.
Chapter 15: Interview with Lynn Parramore for *AlterNet*, 29 September 2014.
Chapter 16: *TripleCrisis*, 28 September 2012.
Chapter 17: *E3: Economics for Equity and the Environment, Policy Brief No. 1*, April 2009.
Chapter 18: 'Investment in Disadvantaged Communities', Memorandum for the Economic and Allocation Advisory Committee, California Air Resources Board and California Environmental Protection Agency, 30 December 2009.
Chapter 19: 'Dividends', Memorandum for the Economic and Allocation Advisory Committee, California Air Resources Board and California Environmental Protection Agency, 30 December 2009.
Chapter 20: *TripleCrisis*, 26 May 2010.

Chapter 21: *TripleCrisis*, 26 May 2011.
Chapter 22: *TripleCrisis*, 27 August 2012.
Chapter 23: *Dollars & Sense*, July 2014.
Chapter 24: *New York Times*, 30 July 2014.
Chapter 25: Political Economy Research Institute, Working Paper No. 188, November 2008.
Chapter 26: Excerpted from 'Distributional Considerations in Climate Policy'. Paper presented at the Annual Conference of the Institute for New Economic Thinking, Paris, April 2015.
Chapter 27: *Los Angeles Times*, 22 December 2014.
Chapter 28: *Scholars Strategy Network*, April 2016.

INDEX

CPSIA information can be obtained
at www.ICGtesting.com
Printed in the USA
JSHW052248120922
30441JS00001B/12